HIDDEN RULES OF CLASS
AT WORK

central massachusetts center for
healthycommunities

A Program of LUK, Inc.
Funded by the MA Dept. of Public Health
44 Front Street, Suite 280
Worcester, MA 01608-1733
www.cmchc.org

Payne, Ruby K., & Krabill, Don L.
    Hidden Rules of Class at Work.185 pp.
    Bibliography pp.179-185.
    ISBN 10: 1-929229-07-0
    ISBN 13: 978-1-929229-07-9

1. Success in business   2. Sociology   3. Title

Ruby K. Payne
Don L. Krabill

HIDDEN RULES OF CLASS
AT WORK

TABLE OF CONTENTS

INTRODUCTION

PURPOSE OF THE BOOK

The purpose of this book is to help those of you who supervise people. This book provides tools for the following:

1. Identification of an individual's strengths and weaknesses by looking at his/her resources.
2. An understanding of how economic class influences opportunities to develop resources.
3. An understanding of how economic class influences – often subtly yet significantly – behaviors that show up in the workplace. (Many of the behaviors an individual uses come out of the economic class in which he/she was raised because survival demanded it.)
4. An understanding of how the levels of an organization reflect the hidden rules of class.
5. Tools that will help you develop employees to function at the level of the organization to which you either have promoted them or at which you expect them to function.
6. Tools for yourself that will assist with your own promotion to the level you wish to achieve.
7. Tools to determine for whom training dollars will have the most payoff.

Here is a mental model that we initially might use:

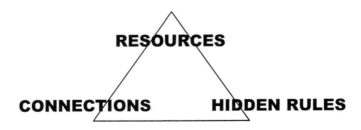

In this oversimplified triangle, an individual brings to an organization three things: resources, connections (relationships), and hidden rules. The organization also has those three things: resources, connections, and hidden rules. The successful fit of the individual into the organization is largely determined by how well these three elements from the individual mesh with those of the organization.

It's important to note that most supervision comes from mid-management types of positions, which generally follow the hidden rules of middle class. This book has no intention of judging one class as better than another. Rather, different realities demand different types of behaviors that, in turn, generate hidden rules. The ability of an individual to *fit* into a work environment and be productive in that environment is crucial to understanding workplace success.

This book's principal objective is to identify and articulate a number of issues that are alive in the workplace – but that seldom have been articulated previously. *Hidden Rules of Class at Work* is not meant to cover all variables in the work setting. Its *raison d'être* is more modest. The book is simply intended to look at how issues of class determine one's ability to survive in the workplace – and to offer the tools necessary to move to a different level of the organization *if one so desires.*

In 1995 I (Ruby Payne) wrote a book titled *A Framework for Understanding Poverty*. The book was written primarily for educators who were trying to deal with social-class issues in the public schools. Several of the participants in the workshops who have a spouse in the corporate environment asked if such a book also could be written for people in business.

Subsequently I teamed up with my cousin, Don Krabill, who owns companies in the United States and England, and we prepared this book.

 **ABOUT THE RESEARCH STUDY …**

Hidden Rules of Class at Work is based on a research study that Don and I did. We developed the resource quotient as an assessment instrument and distributed it to about 250 business people in the United States, targeting mid-management positions or higher. A total of 111 surveys were returned, two of which were incomplete.

The Krabill/Payne Resource Quotient instrument is reliable. Using Cronbach's Coefficient Alpha Scale, the instrument scored .8384 for reliability. (A score of .70 or higher is considered to be very good for this type of instrument.) The Spearman-Brown formula gives the

Krabill/Payne quotient an even more impressive score of .8955 for reliability. (For more details about our research, see the Appendix, along with brief summaries at the end of Chapters 3-12.)

Each chapter gives the research findings for a particular aspect of the instrument, as well as cites other studies that corroborate our findings (see also Research Notes for more of the latter). In addition, each chapter offers interventions that an individual can use to build or strengthen particular resources.

This book is not intended to be "the" definitive statement on the very large topic of resources in the workplace. Rather, its aim is to begin the discussion of how class-related factors and hidden rules impact – often in surprising and significant ways – the working environment in North America.

CHAPTER

1

THE

GOLDEN KEYS

OF

ECONOMIC

REALITIES

ASSESSMENTS

Assessments

To begin to understand the information in this book, it will be helpful for you, the reader, to take the following quizzes and make the following self-assessments.

Could you survive in an unskilled-labor job?
(usually is minimum wage or slightly higher)

1. I know how to physically fight and can hold my own in a fight.
2. I know where the best local bars are.
3. I will quit on the spot if the boss makes me mad.
4. I can go without work for periods of time and survive.
5. I know how to file for unemployment.
6. A phrase I use is: "I was looking for a job when I found this one."
7. I often must take personal phone calls during work time.
8. At work I openly discuss my sex life and the fights I have with family members.
9. If I'm interested sexually in someone at work, I make comments and openly pursue the person.
10. I know how to ask for an advance on my paycheck.
11. I will openly discuss the disagreements I have with my boss or the flaws I see in my boss.
12. I often use casual speech (register) at work.

Could you survive in beginning supervision?
(usually involves responsibility for a group of people without final say about hiring and firing)

1. I can work side by side with the crew to get a job done without losing the authority I have.
2. I know how to stay out of the discussion when everyone else is complaining about the boss.
3. I can anticipate what my boss will want or need.
4. I can respond to written reports in writing.

5. I know how to settle most disagreements or work out compromises without going to the boss.
6. I can decide appropriately which "incidents" the boss needs to know about and which ones he/she doesn't need to know about.
7. I can teach newly hired workers how to do their tasks.
8. I know how to avoid work assignments from bosses other than my own.
9. I know how to deal with "you're one of them" comments from the workers I'm supervising.

Could you survive in mid-management?

(usually involves salary duties and supervisory responsibilities)

1. I know how to sort through paperwork and address the paperwork that has priority.
2. I know which volunteer efforts are most important to the company.
3. I know how to manage the corporate structure above me.
4. I understand the difference between the written goals of the company and the "real" goals.
5. I know how to work the politics of the administrative structure so that the goals of my department can be met.
6. I know which bosses and secretaries (administrative assistants) control the company's actual power structure.
7. I participate in professional development and training programs.
8. I use a time-management system or planner.
9. I make business calls from my car phone or cell phone.
10. I know how to work the company expense accounts so that virtually all of my travel is reimbursed.
11. I can bite my tongue when the boss makes me mad.
12. I know how to set up meeting agendas to meet both my department's needs and to achieve my personal goals.
13. I know the patterns of promotion within the company.
14. I know which subjects can and cannot be discussed at meetings.
15. If I have personal problems, I don't discuss them openly at work.

Could you survive in a corporate executive position?

(usually involves salary, bonus, corporate perks, stock options, and responsibilities that are reported to a board of directors)

1. I know how to negotiate a contract with the appropriate perks for my position (i.e., corporate car leases, cell phones, laptops, office furniture, club memberships).
2. I use corporate residences when I travel.
3. I travel first class or business class – or by corporate jet.
4. My spouse understands how important his/her social role is to my prospects for promotion.
5. I participate in one of these sports: sailing, golf, or tennis – or an exotic sport/activity (i.e., one that requires considerable money, such as scuba diving or hot-air ballooning).
6. I know the best restaurants and clubs in several cities around the world.
7. When traveling, I have favorite hotels in which I know the *concierge,* who advises me on the latest developments in restaurants, clubs, and resorts.
8. I can get tickets to football bowl games, baseball's World Series, NCAA Final Four basketball games, etc., at the last minute.
9. I can select the best wine(s) by maker and by year.
10. I can read a corporate financial statement, spot the omissions, and figure company worth in a short period of time.
11. Whether I "use" or not, I know how to discreetly purchase cocaine and other designer drugs.
12. I understand how important my political, social, and financial connections are to the well-being of the corporation – and spend considerable time maintaining these networks, as well as developing additional connections.
13. I know how to develop and protect my corporate turf.
14. I know which charities and political causes the corporation supports.
15. I have collegial relationships with several members of the board of directors.
16. I understand the imperative nature of both short-term profits and long-term goals.
17. I know how to avoid participating in the bribery systems of other countries.

18. I use my connections to establish business liaisons in other countries.
19. I know how to enhance corporate financials so that our corporation is seen in the best possible light.
20. I know how to protect and secure personal and corporate data.
21. I know how to destroy data, and I know which data should be destroyed.

Could you survive as a self-made millionaire?
(first-generation wealth)

1. I have a high energy level.
2. I have the ability to make connections.
3. I can delegate.
4. I have an innate, "gut" sense about people and/or ideas.
5. I can multitask – manage several tasks or projects simultaneously.
6. I can prioritize my time.
7. I can give up relationships for a period of time in order to more effectively build my company.
8. I identify and use the tools of analytical measurement that track company progress, particularly during periods of fast growth (i.e., percentages vs. numbers).
9. I can live for long periods of time with financial uncertainty, lack of recognition, *and* lack of sleep.

Krabill/Payne Resource Quotient

To complete, use a highlighter and mark the phrases in each category that best describe you.

	0	1	2	3	4
Integrity	Predictably amoral. Destructive to others. Practices deception.	Inconsistent. Unpredictable. No internal compass. Right and wrong are gray areas.	Consistently moral, ethical, and legal. Decides in best interests of self. Rationalizes poor decisions.	Decisions are moral, ethical, and legal. Avoids difficult issues. Is responsible for self but blames others.	Decisions are moral, ethical, and legal. Tough issues are addressed. Accepts responsibility for self and is accountable to others.
Financial	Bills unpaid. Creditors calling.	Paycheck to paycheck. Bills paid late.	More income than bills. Some savings.	Building assets in home. Limited investments.	Has net worth other than home. Many investments.
Emotional	No emotional stamina. Impulsive. Engages in self-destruct-tive behavior (addiction, violence, abusive adult relationships, casual sex).	Moves between voices of child and parent. Blames and accuses. Impulsive. Mood swings.	Uses adult voice except in conflict. Outbursts of anger. Sometimes engages in impulsive behavior.	Uses adult voice in conflict. Avoids conflict. Rarely impulsive.	Uses adult voice in conflict. Confronts, yet maintains relationships. Is not impulsive.
Mental	Relies totally on casual register and non-verbal data to communicate. Not much formal education. Disorganized.	Can read and write formal register. Prefers casual register. Can do basic math. Has difficulty managing time and tasks.	Knows when to use formal register. Has some training beyond high school. Can implement a plan if told how. Knows the what but not the how.	Uses formal register well. Formal education. Can do long-range planning. Knows the what and the how.	Consistently uses formal register well. Knows the what and the why. Initiates and executes plans. Congruence between non-verbals and words.

	0	1	2	3	4
Spiritual destiny	Has no hope. Believes in fate. Choice and consequence are not linked. Discipline is about punishment, penance, and forgiveness.	Believes in good and bad luck. Few choices are considered. Tries not to get caught.	Believes that choices affect destiny. Options are examined. Choices and consequences are linked. Believes in a higher power.	Believes that choices affect destiny. Is affiliated with spiritual, religious, or humanitarian group. Is self-governing. Believes in a higher power.	Thoughts and choices determine destiny. Actively participates in and supports humanitarian causes. Believes in a higher power and purpose larger than self.
Physical	Cannot take care of physical self. Requires assistance. Risky behaviors create health problems.	Can take care of self. Often sick. *Or* can take care of self but does not. Unkempt.	Clean, presentable. Able to take care of self. Mostly healthy.	Attractive. Physically able. Mostly healthy.	Very attractive. Weight, height proportional. Excellent physical health.
Support system	Alone.	Is providing support for limited group of people, which could include friends or family. Tries to build intimacy at work.	Has support system of friends and family. Friends and family may not know appropriate hidden rules of individual's position.	Has support system at work and at home. Knows how to seek help if needed. Friends and family know appropriate hidden rules of individual's position.	Has support system at home, at work, and in community. Has large network of professional colleagues. Can purchase help if needed.
Relation-ships	Uncommitted relationships that are destructive or damaging.	Few bonding relationships of any kind. Perceives self as unlovable.	Several personal relationships. Has several individuals who can be relied upon for help. Is loved.	Many personal and professional relationships. Is loved *and* has someone to love.	Large number of personal and professional relationships. Has been mentored and has mentored others.

	0	1	2	3	4
Hidden rules of class at work	Knows and uses hidden rules of street at work.	Knows and uses hidden rules of hourly wages at work.	Knows and uses hidden rules that members of mid-management follow at work.	Knows and uses hidden rules that officials at executive level follow at work. Knows hidden rules of country club.	Knows and uses hidden rules that are followed in corporate boardroom and with charities. Understands organizational, social, and business pedigree and hierarchy.
Desire and persistence	Low energy. Not motivated. Does not want to be promoted. Dislikes learning. Quits often.	Selective energy but maybe not at work. Works for the money. Does not seek promotion. Avoids training. Gives up easily.	Steady energy. Motivated by need to be personally right. Controls information. Wants to be promoted for the power. Attends training.	High energy. Motivated by need to be organization-ally correct. Seeks out training. Promotion or rewards desired for recognition.	High energy. Motivated by challenge. Promotion or rewards reflect excellence. Constantly learning on his/her own. Very persistent.

Economic realities (class) create rules by which people live. The context or the environment shapes their thinking and their behaviors. Many times these "rules" are hidden, i.e., they're almost never articulated at a conscious level. Hidden rules are those unspoken, cueing mechanisms used to determine whether you do or do not belong. Often these rules are absolute and are used to identify intelligence. To be sure, there are hidden rules with regard to race, religion, and region of the country, but such rules also exist with regard to economic class.

Each of us is like a piece of fabric. Some threads go vertically (the warp), and some threads go horizontally (the woof). The warp threads represent cultural and racial issues. The woof threads are those contexts that are cross-cultural, such as economics and aging. These contexts, because of cause and effect, tend to create patterns that are fairly universal.

If I must work 15 hours a day just to survive and have enough food to keep me alive, then that is what I will do. But it means that virtually all my time will be spent on survival and those aspects of life that facilitate my survival. Time and energy to devote to learning, to the artistic, to the abstract will be severely limited.

In the world of work, individuals come to the workplace with many different fabrics, woven through a combination of contexts. Psychologist Jerome Bruner states that all intelligence is related to context and task. The hidden rules each individual follows shape his/her behaviors and, inevitably, the workplace. And, it must be noted, the hidden rules of the workplace also shape individuals.

These hidden rules affect who gets promoted and who does not. They impact to an even greater degree the ability of the organization to function well. This book not only explains the hidden rules regarding economic realities, it also outlines the tools necessary for being promoted — and ways in which individuals and corporations can begin to identify the hidden aspects of promotion.

CHAPTER

2

SURPRISE!

HERE I AM

WHAT ARE MY RESOURCES?

What Are My Resources?

Resources make a big difference in the ability of an individual to be supervised and the ways in which an employer can provide support and assistance to employees.

Generally, as a rule of thumb, the greater the *net worth* of an individual, the greater his/her access to resources. Some resources, however, cannot be purchased. It isn't possible to purchase genuine relationships that are nurturing and caring. It is possible, though, to buy attention.

Krabill/Payne Resource Quotient

	0	1	2	3	4
Integrity	Predictably amoral. Destructive to others. Practices deception.	Inconsistent. Unpredictable. No internal compass. Right and wrong are gray areas.	Consistently moral, ethical, and legal. Decides in best interests of self. Rationalizes poor decisions.	Decisions are moral, ethical and legal. Avoids difficult issues. Is responsible for self but blames others.	Decisions are moral, ethical, and legal. Tough issues are addressed. Accepts responsibility for self and is accountable to others.
Financial	Bills unpaid. Creditors calling.	Paycheck to paycheck. Bills paid late.	More income than bills. Some savings.	Building assets in home. Limited investments.	Has net worth other than home. Many investments.

	0	1	2	3	4
Emotional	No emotional stamina. Impulsive. Engages in self-destruct-ive behavior (addiction, violence, abusive adult relationships, casual sex).	Moves between voices of child and parent. Blames and accuses. Impulsive. Mood swings.	Uses adult voice except in conflict. Outbursts of anger. Sometimes engages in impulsive behavior.	Uses adult voice in conflict. Avoids conflict. Rarely impulsive.	Uses adult voice in conflict. Confronts, yet maintains relationships. Is not impulsive.
Mental	Relies totally on casual register and non-verbal data to communicate. Not much formal education. Disorganized.	Can read and write formal register. Prefers casual register. Can do basic math. Has difficulty managing time and tasks.	Knows when to use formal register. Has some training beyond high school. Can implement a plan if told how. Knows the <u>what</u> but not the <u>how</u>.	Uses formal register well. Formal education. Can do long-range planning. Knows the <u>what</u> *and* the <u>how</u>.	Consistently uses formal register well. Knows the <u>what</u> and the <u>why</u>. Initiates and executes plans. Congruence between non-verbals and words.
Spiritual destiny	Has no hope. Believes in fate. Choices and consequences are not linked. Discipline is about punishment, penance, and forgiveness.	Believes in good and bad luck. Few choices are considered. Tries not to get caught.	Believes that choices affect destiny. Options are examined. Choices and consequences are linked. Believes in a higher power.	Believes that choices affect destiny. Is affiliated with spiritual, religious, or humanitarian group. Is self-governing. Believes in a higher power.	Thoughts and choices determine destiny. Actively participates in and supports humanitarian causes. Believes in a higher power and purpose larger than self.
Physical	Cannot take care of physical self. Requires assistance. Risky behaviors create health problems.	Can take care of self. Often sick. *Or* can take care of self but does not. Unkempt.	Clean, presentable. Able to take care of self. Mostly healthy.	Attractive. Physically able. Mostly healthy.	Very attractive. Weight, height proportional. Excellent physical health.

	0	1	2	3	4
Support system	Alone.	Is providing support for limited group of people, which could include friends or family. Tries to build intimacy at work.	Has support system of friends and family. Friends and family may not know appropriate hidden rules of individual's position.	Has support system at work and at home. Knows how to seek help if needed. Friends and family know appropriate hidden rules of individual's position.	Has support system at home, at work, and in community. Has large network of professional colleagues. Can purchase help if needed.
Relation-ships	Uncommitted relationships that are destructive or damaging.	Few bonding relationships of any kind. Perceives self as unlovable.	Several personal relation-ships. Has several individuals who can be relied upon for help. Is loved.	Many personal and professional relationships. Is loved *and* has someone to love.	Large number of personal and professional relationships. Has been mentored and has mentored others.
Hidden rules of class at work	Knows and uses hidden rules of street at work.	Knows and uses hidden rules of hourly wages at work.	Knows and uses hidden rules that members of mid-management follow at work.	Knows and uses hidden rules that officials at executive level follow at work. Knows hidden rules of country club.	Knows and uses hidden rules that are followed in corporate boardroom and with charities. Understands organizational, social, and business pedigree and hierarchy.
Desire and persistence	Low energy. Not motivated. Does not want to be promoted. Dislikes learning. Quits often.	Selective energy but maybe not at work. Works for the money. Does not seek promotion. Avoids training. Gives up easily.	Steady energy. Motivated by need to be personally right. Controls information. Wants to be promoted for the power. Attends training.	High energy. Motivated by need to be organization-ally correct. Seeks out training. Promotion or rewards desired for recognition.	High energy. Motivated by challenge. Promotion or rewards reflect excellence. Constantly learning on his/her own. Very persistent.

A SCORE UNDER 10 indicates an individual who will need a great deal of supervision.
A SCORE OF 11-17 indicates an individual who is inconsistent. Performance is uneven.
A SCORE OF 18-PLUS indicates an individual with a great deal of potential. The total score will
    be related to specific strengths and weaknesses.

Brief Discussion of Each Characteristic

The first item that must be assessed is the individual's level of integrity. Regardless of skill level or intelligence, integrity is *the* key issue in promotion. It determines the amount of supervision an individual will need and, likewise, his/her ability to supervise. No person or corporation can be successful over time without integrity, an attribute that affects every aspect of the business. An individual without integrity who nonetheless is promoted eventually creates difficulties for himself/herself or for the company. At some point a decision will be required from the employee that will test his/her integrity. Failure to maintain honesty ultimately shows up in harassment charges, tax issues, lawsuits, fraud, court cases, and other problems. In research (Kouzes & Posner, 1993) in which 1,500 managers throughout the U.S. identified the key characteristics of leaders, integrity was overwhelmingly the No. 1 choice. Time and time again managers stated that without integrity there is no chance for genuine leadership.

Most employers spend a great deal of time assessing the mental, physical, and motivational resources of prospective employees. In job interviews some employers are learning to watch for hidden rules of class (the ones that are articulated). *To be promoted to mid-management, one must know the hidden rules of middle class. To be promoted to the executive level, one must know the hidden rules of wealth.*

But the resources that are essential to the stability and evenness of daily performance are rarely articulated. These resources are financial, emotional, support systems, beliefs about spirituality and destiny, and nurturing/caring relationships. The lack of – or disruption of – these resources creates a roller-coaster ride for the individual, who then brings the roller coaster into the workplace and disrupts it through uneven performance, mood swings, absenteeism, mindlessness, rage, and cognitive distortion.

It is the unpredictability of performance that often creates safety issues, litigation, and conflict. In the last several years, emotional issues in the workplace have begun to be addressed (*Emotional Intelligence,* Daniel Goleman, 1995), along with spiritual/destiny issues, the need for a support system, and nurturing relationships (Stephen Covey). The Krabill/Payne Resource Quotient instrument is a quick way of determining one's areas of personal strength and weakness.

Case Studies

Here are six case studies for you to analyze.

AUDREY

Audrey is brilliant. She has a Ph.D. and has written two books. She has been hired by your human resources division as an organizational consultant. She is single, has never been married, and has a large reddish birthmark that covers the left side of her face. Audrey, 38, is highly intelligent, funny, and entertaining, but she also can be acerbic, sarcastic, and bitter.

Her life revolves around her work. She has a 10-year-old son. Because of her volatile personality Audrey changes housekeepers often. Sometimes when she's without a housekeeper, she must take her son with her to work or rearrange the days she does consulting. She gets rave reviews from most audiences for her presentations. For her technical, long-term interventions, people either love her or hate her.

Her personal finances appear to be chaotic and troubled. Audrey needs $10,000 a month after taxes just to run her household and pay the help she hires. She has double-billed at least one client but, in the ensuing discussion, indicated it was a mistake. Clients periodically complain about how much she charges for expenses.

In an attempt to get work from one client, Audrey initially explained what she could bring to his organization. When she realized that his firm didn't really need her services, she broke down and cried about her financial situation. When the client indicated that he didn't have the budget to give her work – and also had concerns about issues shared by some of his directors – Audrey proceeded to criticize the directors.

Audrey sees the company where she works as "family" and tries very hard to build relationships with colleagues – to the point that her intensity eventually puts off most of her co-workers. She is quick to orchestrate pressure against anyone who isn't loyal to her current group.

Audrey is a driven individual. Her production output is tremendous. She is currently shopping for a publisher for her next book. She develops materials quickly, seemingly "overnight," but she isn't always careful about the sources. As she says, "I give and I take; it's only fair."

YOU ARE THE SUPERVISOR

Recently you have been peppered with complaints about Audrey. Several of her fellow consultants have indicated that her comments to them have been quite inappropriate and out of line. One colleague, whom you highly respect, refuses to work with Audrey again. Several of Audrey's co-workers are concerned about the company reputation as Audrey works with clients. Another consultant is supportive of Audrey but is concerned because of Audrey's private criticism of company products.

Audrey is still within your corporation's three-month probationary period and can be released. She has been in your office three times this week. The first time she cried about her finances and asked if could she have an advance. The second time she requested a change in technical-assistance days because of her housekeeper. The third time she came to you because she's pushing you to have the company publish a manuscript she hasn't finished writing. You suspect that she's pressuring you largely because she wants to prove to a former colleague at another company that she can be published again.

Furthermore, she tells you that she can transform her financial future — *if* she has your support. You calculate that, in the two months Audrey has been with the company, you have given her more time than you normally give other consultants in a year.

Using the number system of the Krabill/Payne Resource Quotient, assess Audrey's resources.

Integrity	
Financial	
Emotional	
Mental	
Spiritual	
Physical	
Support system	
Relationships	
Hidden rules	
Desire	
TOTAL	

RON

Ron came from a much larger  international corporation to work for the company as a sales representative. He says the bureaucracy of a larger organization isn't for him. Quite handsome, Ron, 29, was college educated with a degree in business. He sometimes works into conversations the fact that he was a basketball star in college. He is currently an active tennis player.

For Ron, who is still highly competitive, getting the sale is everything. So an accurate representation of the product is not an overall concern. Promises are made but frequently broken.

Ron has a lovely wife and two children. Yet when he refers to his son and daughter, it's as though they're pets or objects, and he spends little time with his family. He mentions that he was adopted and, in his case, doesn't have close relationships with his extended family. He makes friends rapidly and has a large number of acquaintances, though he doesn't seem to be able to maintain many long-term relationships. Ron generally does something to anger someone, and then he or they move on. He feels that others should accept him for who he is (yes, duplicity and all) because that's simply the way he is. He appears to believe that somehow or other he will work his way through the maze of life: finding openings …

banging into walls and finding another opening … hitting dead ends …

retreating quickly and starting over.

Ron also appears to view "hitting on" women as a competitive sport

and, if attending a trade show, he will spend long hours in the evening

partying and drinking. But colleagues say this about Ron: In the morning

he's always up and ready to work.

Ron is driven to make money, even though he usually seems short of

it. He has many of the trappings of success – nice house, car, etc. – but

often requests advances on his commissions and salaries.

YOU ARE THE SUPERVISOR

The complaints against Ron are mounting. There's a discrepancy

between warehouse counts of inventory and Ron's accounting. Customers

are calling to complain about products that aren't working. You've asked

Ron to double-check the shelf life of the materials. You've also issued a

company recall of a series of serial numbers that seem defective. Then you

discover that the complaints are coming only from Ron's warehouses.

Finally, you send Ron to a trade show and go to the warehouse

yourself. You find several of the recalled serial numbers reboxed and an

order ready for shipment. In the next week you find several products that were recalled, have been reboxed, and sold again. The billing has not gone through the company.

You confront Ron. His response is to deny it. You fire him anyway. With the facts clearly laid out on the table, he says, "You do what you have to do, man."

Using the number system of the Krabill/Payne Resource Quotient, assess Ron's resources:

Integrity	
Financial	
Emotional	
Mental	
Spiritual	
Physical	
Support system	
Relationships	
Hidden rules	
Desire	
TOTAL	

HARVEY

Harvey came to our company 20 years ago as a technician paid by the hour. He's a 7-to-4 type of guy and openly states that fact. Highly skilled, he's very good at his job but is somewhat overweight and rather nondescript in appearance. Periodically Harvey, 54, will get involved in a physical-fitness fad, but he doesn't stay with it.

He and his second wife, Sylvia, are comfortable financially. They have a nice home, plus a second residence in Florida. His wife works as a Realtor and also has inherited some money, which they've invested. Harvey and Sylvia head for Florida a couple of times a year. Due to his seniority he gets six weeks of vacation a year; he and his wife spend a month in Florida most winters.

At work, Harvey wants to be perceived as fair and honest, going to great lengths to be seen as "defender of the oppressed." When there's a grievance to be aired, fellow employees tend to seek out Harvey for his sympathetic ear. But not wanting to rock the boat and jeopardize his own position, Harvey rarely does anything about the complaints. Because he is such a repository for griping and gossip (but without action), some in the company call Harvey "the little old woman."

He is known to carry grudges for weeks; he and his wife often have long periods of time when they won't talk to each other. Another example: Over a period of years Harvey wouldn't speak with his brother. Often the issue was trivial. In discussion, Harvey steadfastly maintained that he was right and that his brother would "come around." Harvey also has little contact with the four grown children from his first marriage. As he says, "They don't understand me and, if they won't make the effort, then there's no reason for me to have anything to do with them."

YOU ARE THE SUPERVISOR

This week one of your employees, Helen, tells you in the break room about Harvey and Sylvia's card party over the weekend. (They often host such parties.) Helen tells you that several members of the work crew were there, and they're angry that a fellow employee, Ray, may become their next boss (company gossip). It had been announced on Friday that you have been promoted, effective in two weeks, and your position will be open. Helen again: "Harvey says you're the only boss he'll ever have. He's loyal to the one who hires him." Helen also tells you about the ruckus that Harvey has vowed to raise – and all the things Harvey and the others will do to Ray if he takes your position.

Helen then puts in a good word for Harvey, saying he would be an ideal supervisor because he cares about people, and everyone knows he'd be the best boss. You, however, know that Harvey has refused to go to the last three training opportunities and that he simply won't confront. Furthermore, just last week you had to talk to him privately about a sexually suggestive remark he made to a 30-year-old female colleague. When you confronted Harvey, he said, "Well, that was a compliment! What's wrong with *her*?" And when you told him he couldn't do that again – that he must change his behavior – he said, "If girls don't know a compliment when they hear one, well, I can't do anything about that."

Using the number system of the Krabill/Payne Resource Quotient, assess Harvey's resources:

Integrity	
Financial	
Emotional	
Mental	
Spiritual	
Physical	
Support system	
Relationships	
Hidden rules	
Desire	
TOTAL	

ZELDA

Zelda is a welfare-to-work employee whom you hired to do receptionist work and to enter data into the computer. Because she got pregnant at 16 and dropped out of school, Zelda, 25, doesn't have a diploma but does have a GED. Her son is now 8 years old. She cares very much about him and wants him to do well in school. Her mother never worked outside the home; her sisters still don't. When Zelda sets her mind to it, she's quick and sharp at learning new skills. Astute about finances, Zelda know how to manage money, though in her present circumstances she lives from paycheck to paycheck. She's 5 feet tall and weighs around 200 pounds.

She usually has reliable transportation; her mother keeps her son when there's a day-care problem. Zelda has several friends and spends a portion of the workday talking with them. She gets her tasks done but often shows up five to 10 minutes late. You've worked with her on her phone-answering skills. Periodically she'll lapse into answering the phone by saying, "Hey."

Zelda will do whatever is asked – if she understands the reasons why. Zelda also will tell you exactly what she thinks of just about any situation or person and will seldom back down.

YOU ARE THE OWNER OF THE COMPANY

The business is growing, and you recently offered to financially cover classes for Zelda at the local junior college, but she turns it down. Her comment: "I ain't got no time for that." But you know that she often goes out with friends in the evening. When you asked why she wasn't interested in taking classes, Zelda replied, "Hey, I wouldn't be working at all if I didn't have to."

Zelda came to you last week and explained yet again why she would need to leave work early: this time to take her mother to the doctor. She asks off early an average of once a week. Also, her boyfriend was in an accident two weeks ago with her car and, during the workday last Thursday, she had to get a ride to take care of things pertaining to her car.

Because of the rapid growth of the company, increasingly you note that Zelda is getting behind, and her tasks aren't getting done. To help lighten your own workload, you recently hired a supervisor. Zelda balks at working with the new supervisor. Zelda tells you, "I like you; I'll do the work for you. You're my boss, not Frieda." You tell her that she must work with the new supervisor. Later that day Zelda quits.

Using the number system of the Krabill/Payne Resource Quotient, assess Zelda's resources:

Integrity	
Financial	
Emotional	
Mental	
Spiritual	
Physical	
Support system	
Relationships	
Hidden rules	
Desire	
TOTAL	

SANDRA

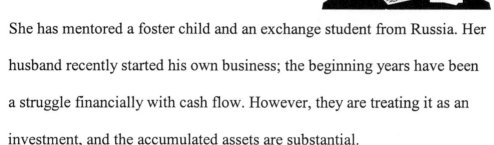

Sandra is attractive, 5-foot-4, and 130 pounds. She is 43, married, and has never had children. She has mentored a foster child and an exchange student from Russia. Her husband recently started his own business; the beginning years have been a struggle financially with cash flow. However, they are treating it as an investment, and the accumulated assets are substantial.

Sandra has two master's degrees, is bilingual, and is well organized. She can plan *and* execute just about any task given to her. For Sandra, it's more important to be respected than liked, though virtually all who work with her do both. She has a way of confronting people that is clear and to the point, yet in a manner that respects the personhood of the individual. In general, individuals rarely leave a confrontation with Sandra feeling that they were mistreated.

She loves her work, and her eyes sparkle when she talks about the issues at work that she has been addressing. For Sandra, a problem is an opportunity. People fascinate her, and she cares deeply about them. Very persistent, Sandra will see a job through to the end.

YOU ARE ON THE INTERVIEWING COMMITTEE

Sandra is up for promotion to a vice president's position. You will be her boss. You know that Sandra was the individual who made her former boss (an inordinately difficult man who has since been fired) look very good. You know that Sandra never said anything derogatory about her boss. And with your ear to the ground lately, you can't find a soul who has anything bad to say about Sandra. Furthermore, you've had four people call you and ask that you please consider Sandra for vice president.

Your concern is this: You haven't seen any indication from Sandra that she understands *systems* issues. Furthermore, you know very little about her spouse. Sandra works 12- to 15-hour days. Will she be able to shift a significant portion of her time to making connections and monitoring systems that will be required at that level of the organization? You can't afford to promote someone who can't do these things. You know that Sandra grew up middle class, and you know that she and her husband are not members of any clubs, except for an exercise club that she visits daily. Last week you asked her to join you for a round of golf, and she just laughed and said, "Who has time to chase a little white ball?" Also, because she has been more of a mentor to her bosses than they have to her, Sandra has not had any respected executive mentor her in the seven years she has been with the company.

Using the number system of the Krabill/Payne Resource Quotient, assess Sandra's resources:

Integrity	
Financial	
Emotional	
Mental	
Spiritual	
Physical	
Support system	
Relationships	
Hidden rules	
Desire	
TOTAL	

TERESA

Teresa was hired as an assembly line worker in a factory. English was her second language when she came to the United States 25 years ago. Attractive and always stylish and colorful in dress, she has great manual dexterity. Her reading and writing skills are somewhat limited, and she still has difficulty taking directions in written English. But if you show her how to do something, she can do it immediately.

Teresa, 48, was married three times – the first two to very difficult men whom she supported financially. In addition, she had several live-in boyfriends along the way. Her third marriage – to Chico – helped her gain ground and reach financial stability, i.e., she could live from paycheck to paycheck. They divorced two years ago. She has three grown children, all by different fathers; two of her grandchildren live with her, and she has taken in foster children from time to time. Teresa was raised in extreme poverty and views her life with a high degree of fatalism, yet she is active in her neighborhood church. In short, her belief system seems to be a mix of roll-the-dice fate and Christian faith.

When Teresa's children had difficulties, she was always there to support them, just as she readily helps anyone in need. Of Teresa, people say, "She has a heart of gold." Not surprisingly, she has a network of people she can count on.

Teresa's emotional responses to colleagues vary, but she maintains great loyalty to the person who hired her.

YOU ARE THE SUPERVISOR

Teresa came to you recently to tell you there was a problem with one of the products. When you asked her what was wrong, she said, "I can't say exactly, but I can feel it." That is all she could articulate for you. You have learned you must be careful with your comments to Teresa. She is very proud, and any negative comment is usually viewed as personal criticism. In fact, when specifics of a product were discussed a few months ago, she told you it was "close enough." When you explained that close enough was not good enough, she seemed offended.

Using the number system of the Krabill/Payne Resource Quotient, assess Teresa's resources.

Integrity	
Financial	
Emotional	
Mental	

Spiritual	
Physical	
Support system	
Relationships	
Hidden rules	
Desire	
TOTAL	

www.ahaprocess.com

Debriefing the Resource Quotient

Here you can get an overview of our assessment of the resources of each person in the preceding case studies. You may wish to see how your assessments compare with ours.

Resource	Audrey	Ron	Harvey	Zelda	Sandra	Teresa
Integrity	2	0	3	4	4	2
Financial	1	1	4	2	4	1
Emotional	1	0	2	2	4	2
Mental	4	3	2	1	4	0
Spiritual	2	1	2	2	4	*
Physical	2	4	2	2	4	3
Support system	1	1	3	2	4	2
Relationships	2	1	3	2	3	2
Hidden rules	2	2	1	1	2	1
Desire	4	2	1	1	4	1
TOTAL	21	15	23	19	37	14

* See "DEBRIEFING TERESA" on page 53 for the explanation of this asterisk.

DEBRIEFING AUDREY

There is a saying in the workplace: "Hire on skills, fire on behavior." That would be true for Audrey. This is a case of an individual who is brilliant and driven. But because of her lack of resources emotionally and lack of a support system, she is very needy. Her ability to manipulate people is formidable. She attempts to create intimacy at work, i.e., "I'll verbally protect you if you are loyal to me." The amount of time taken from work to build intimacy and "family" is considerable – not to mention the "he said, she said, you said" that comes from the loyalty squabbles. Because of Audrey's great emotional needs and her lack of a predictable support system, her work performance is quite uneven. That makes it very difficult from a supervisory angle.

The questions that must be asked about Audrey are as follows: (1) Do her intellectual assets outweigh her emotional liabilities? (2) Do I have enough time to supervise Audrey? And (3) if I really need Audrey's intellect, what can I do as a supervisor to create a surrogate support system?

If you were the supervisor, what would you do with Audrey?

DEBRIEFING RON

Ron is a classic case of no integrity. Basically, if an individual comes in with an integrity score of 0 or 1, he/she should not be hired. Or, if such an individual already is working for the company, he/she should be placed in a position with no access to cash and budgets – and with no supervisory duties.

Ron is an example of a person who has neither the integrity nor the emotional resources to make sound decisions. All his decision making will be skewed. Stories and reports will have major omissions. The corporate training program may need to include a course in ethics and ethical decision making, though even that may not be enough to turn someone like Ron around.

DEBRIEFING HARVEY

Harvey is a solid employee but can't be promoted because of his lack of emotional resources *and* lack of desire. Harvey really doesn't want the added responsibility of supervision.

If you are Harvey's supervisor, these are the questions that must be asked: Is there a way to make Harvey more responsible about his rescuing and gossiping? Is there an incentive that will motivate him to attend training?

DEBRIEFING ZELDA

Zelda is a good example of someone who doesn't know the hidden rules of middle class and therefore the workplace. In generational poverty, responsibility is defined as loyalty to a person, whereas in middle class, responsibility is defined as accountability for a task or standard. Zelda is baffled that her boss would hire someone else to whom she must answer.

Zelda could be promoted were she willing to go return to school, but relationships are crucial to survival, and she chooses not to give the time to schooling because it would take away from relationships. The reasons Zelda can make the transition from welfare to work are her mental resources and her support system. But her desire to make the transition is limited.

A question for the supervisor is: Do I have the time to mentor Zelda?

DEBRIEFING SANDRA

Sandra is exceptional. She is a classic example of an individual who has all the resources *except* knowledge of the hidden rules of the wealth, which govern the executive level. She doesn't know these because she hasn't had a mentor who will teach them to her. It's very evident in her response to playing golf. Sandra doesn't understand the significance of that request. An aspect of mid-management that is crucial to success is task completion. But at the executive level, it's the ability to make connections and identify the strategic processes and infrastructures that will move the organization forward. The question Sandra's potential boss must ask is: How can I find out if this is a teachable area for her prior to promoting her? What would you do?

DEBRIEFING TERESA

Teresa is an example of a person who has come from extreme poverty where daily survival is the first and foremost rule. So for her, work is the most predictable and stable aspect of her life. In the chart on p. 49 "Spiritual" is marked with an asterisk (*) because here the chart doesn't work well. Teresa's strong religious affiliations give her a belief in a higher power, but due to her lack of education she believes that everything is God's will. If she believes and prays, God will take care of her, no matter how many "crosses she has to bear." Like many individuals who grew up in extreme poverty, her opportunities to be formally educated were significantly reduced. Also, because of Teresa's lack of education, her ability to think and speak analytically about the job is limited. One thing formal education provides is the capacity for viewing facts and factors separately from emotion – at an issue level. Teresa cannot do that.

 **HOW CAN I USE THIS INFORMATION?**

When you are having difficulty with an employee, you …	~ can do a quick private assessment of his/her resources.
When you are denied a promotion, you …	~ can ask your boss or a colleague to assess your resources.
When you are determining training needs, you …	~ can do a quick assessment of the resource areas that need to be developed.

PLEASE NOTE: The development of resources is often closely tied to economic class. The real issue in economic class is the opportunities that one has for developing resources. If I'm working 15 hours a day to stay alive, I can't develop as many connections. I don't have time to learn to ski, golf, swim, and sail. I may not have time for formal education. If a car isn't available, I won't learn to drive. Furthermore, if I don't have a support system, I can't devote as much time to advancing at work. And the list goes on.

HOW CAN I IDENTIFY AND AUGMENT RESOURCES?

Each of the ensuing chapters takes one resource and looks at it in depth. Listed at the end of each chapter are specific suggestions about ways to build or enhance that particular resource, along with a brief summary of the Krabill/Payne research on that characteristic.

CHAPTER

3

WHY DO I FEEL LIKE I DON'T BELONG?

HIDDEN RULES OF CLASS

Hidden rules of class at work	Knows and uses hidden rules of street at work.	Knows and uses hidden rules of hourly wages at work.	Knows and uses hidden rules that members of mid-management follow at work.	Knows and uses hidden rules that officials at executive level follow at work. Knows hidden rules of country club.	Knows and uses hidden rules that are followed in corporate boardroom and with charities. Understands organizational, social, and business pedigree and hierarchy

Hidden Rules of Class

Hidden rules by economic class are an integral part of the workplace. Hidden rules are the unspoken cues and habits of a group. Distinct cueing systems exist between and among groups and economic classes. Generally in America this notion is clearly recognized for racial and ethnic groups but not for economic class.

Technically there are five economic classes: generational poverty (or welfare poverty – has been in place for at least two generations), working class, middle class, new money, and old money. The biggest difference between new money and old money is that new money is about income, while old money is about net worth and connections.

Having money or not having money creates cause-and-effect situations that result in a fairly common set of hidden rules. For example, if a person has been born into the middle class and his/her parents were also, then most decision making in that household revolves around three issues: work, achievement, and material security. Things tend to be considered possessions, and the hidden rule about money is: "I don't ask you for money, and you don't ask me."

But if you lived in wealth for two generations, there would be a great deal of material security, and considerable time and effort would be devoted to keeping it and growing it. Decision making would revolve around these three elements: financial connections, social connections, and political connections. Connections would keep the person safe *and* help him/her make more money. Possessions would be one-of-a-kind art objects, legacies, pedigrees, and, yes, bloodlines. The hidden rule about money would be that money per se is not discussed – investments, yes – but not money itself.

Another hidden rule that comes out of this need for safety is that in wealth, one doesn't introduce oneself. A person is introduced in this fashion: "This is so-and-so of such-and-such family or firm." Immediately the person is introduced, along with the connection. If an individual is introduced this way, "This is so-and-so, a very dear personal friend," then the unstated understanding is that the person has no connections of note.

But if an individual has been in poverty two generations or more, he/she has very few things, and daily life is about survival. Time is devoted to survival. Decision making revolves around three things: survival, relationships, and entertainment. That's why, in generational poverty (two generations or more), people almost always have a TV and a VCR, even if very little else is available – because entertainment is so important. The reason entertainment is so important is that poverty is painful, and humor is a way to mitigate the pain.

When there are limited material things, and life is about survival, then virtually the only possession one has is people. And when people become possessions, the rules change. That's why the physical fights over people are so intense – the person is a possession. That's why being educated is often feared in generational poverty because when people get educated they usually leave. That's why the put-downs for getting training or getting educated are so intense from those who come out of generational poverty. When upwardly mobile individuals from the poverty culture aren't at work, the comments to them in the neighborhood go something like this: "You're gettin' above your raisings." Or: "You're trying to be white." And that's why, in generational poverty, responsibility is defined as loyalty to a relationship.

What about those who are in between? They are the first generation to be part of a group. Or they're moving from one class to the next. Or they had a parent from generational poverty and one from middle class. Or they had a parent die, or there was a divorce, and the household went from a middle-class lifestyle to one of poverty. This is sometimes termed situational poverty. Those people tend to follow a mixed set of rules – partly based on what they grew up with and partly based on what they're moving toward. Which rules are followed can be determined by the general economic environment, gender, and rules used by the most influential parent.

Hidden Rules in General

HIDDEN RULES AMONG CLASSES			
	Poverty	**Middle Class**	**Wealth**
Possessions	People.	Things.	One-of-a-kind objects, legacies, pedigrees.
Money	To be used, spent.	To be managed.	To be conserved, invested.
Personality	Is for entertainment. Sense of humor is highly valued.	Is for acquisition and stability Achievement is highly valued	Is for connections. Financial, political, and social connections are highly valued.
Social emphasis	Social inclusion of people he/she likes.	Emphasis is on self-governance and self-sufficiency.	Emphasis is on social exclusion.
Food	Key question: Did you have enough? Quantity important.	Key question. Did you like it? Quality important	Key question: Was it presented well? Presentation important
Clothing	Clothing valued for individual style and expression of personality.	Clothing valued for its quality and acceptance into norm of middle class. Label important.	Clothing valued for its artistic sense and expression. Designer important.
Time	Present most important. Decisions made for moment based on feelings or survival	Future most important. Decisions made against future ramifications.	Traditions and history most important Decisions made partially on basis of tradition and decorum.
Education	Valued and revered as abstract but not as reality.	Crucial for climbing success ladder and making money.	Necessary tradition for making and maintaining connections.
Destiny	Believes in fate Cannot do much to mitigate chance.	Believes in choice. Can change future with good choices now.	Noblesse oblige.
Language	Casual register. Language is about survival.	Formal register. Language is about negotiation.	Formal register. Language is about networking.
Family structure	Tends to be matriarchal.	Tends to be patriarchal.	Depends on who has money.
World view	Sees world in terms of local setting.	Sees world in terms of national setting.	Sees world in terms of international view.
Love	Love and acceptance conditional, based on whether individual is liked.	Love and acceptance conditional and based largely on achievement.	Love and acceptance conditional and related to social standing and connections.
Driving force	Survival, relationships, entertainment.	Work, achievement.	Financial, political, social connections.
Humor	About people and sex	About situations.	About social faux pas.

In many ways, these hidden rules of class then carry over to the organization and the corporation.

Hidden Rules at Three Main Levels

A common lament in the workplace: "It isn't fair." A job is open, individuals are up for promotion, and the job goes to someone else. A woman is being considered for an executive position. She and her husband are invited out to dinner. He isn't wearing a tie to the fashionable restaurant, and his table manners aren't quite up to snuff. After the meal is over, the applicant and her husband leave. One executive looks at the other and says, "She married *him*? Forget her."

The economic rules of class play themselves out in the workplace, throughout the levels of the organization. To be effective in mid-management, one must know the hidden rules of middle class. To handle the executive level of an organization, one must know the hidden rules of wealth. For those who are self-employed or independent contractors, knowledge of all sets of hidden rules is extremely beneficial. This is particularly true for those in sales.

The Three Levels

Often in the workplace one will hear among blue-collar employees comments such as these about the boss: "All he does is push paper. That man couldn't handle a *real* job." At the middle level, comments about the boss will include: "All he does is play golf and have two-hour lunches!"

And at the executive level, comments are either about the board of directors or about mid-management: "Can't they ever get accurate and timely information?"

Each level of the organization uses its own hidden rules to make judgments. There is a progression. Generally one must be able to take care of the mid-management tasks in order to move up to the executive level. Sometimes one must be able to do the unskilled-labor tasks in order to move into mid-management.

ISSUE	UNSKILLED LABOR	BEGINNING SUPERVISION	MID-MANAGEMENT	EXECUTIVE LEVEL
Knowledge level	What I can do	What I can get others to do	What I know	Who I know
Responsibilities	Completion of tasks.	Completion of Group tasks. Recommendations about hiring and firing.	Completion of projects and implementation of processes. Authority to hire and fire.	Identification of systems, products, services, and processes within business unit and among other related business units.
Connections	Connections/ camaraderie within group.	With your immediate boss and the group you are supervising	Internal connections up, down, and across organization crucial to success.	External connections vital to success of business unit.
Protocol/culture	Accepted norms of immediate working group.	Mix of what the boss wants and the norms of the group	Corporate hierarchy observed and followed.	National and often international social and business protocol observed and followed.
Financial	Only as it relates to specific tasks.	Only as it relates to group task	Departmental budget.	Profit and loss of business unit. Global strategic sales/revenues.
Planning	Daily, if any.	Planning for group tasks and task delegation.	Weekly to annual. Project management.	Strategic. Quarterly to multi-year.
Time commitment	For hours paid.	Some overtime.	50-60 hours a week.	Position involves spouse, social activities, and extensive travel 60-80 hours a week.
Schooling	High school diploma or less.	High school or some college.*	Often a couple of years of college or college degree.	Often MBA.
Relocation	Not required.	Not required.	May be required.	Required.
Technical expertise	Not required but desirable.	Recommended.	Use of specific software applications required.	Understanding and use of technical systems as they relate to strategic and financial success of business unit.

ISSUE	UNSKILLED LABOR	BEGINNING SUPERVISION	MID-MANAGEMENT	EXECUTIVE LEVEL
Communication	Mostly spoken, some written.	Responds in writing to written reports.	Produces written reports. Makes reports/ presentations to peers, customers, subordinates, and executive level.	Analyzes corporate documents for effect/purpose. Makes reports/ presentations to stakeholders.
Spouse or significant other	Does not matter.	Does not matter.	Helpful but not crucial to career success.	Often determines whether promotion is given or not. Seen to reflect on person's judgment. Is reflection of personal choice.
Appearance	Needs to be somewhat clean.	Clean and presentable.	Wears good-quality clothing that follows company norms and expectations. Clothing is pressed, neat, and clean.	Look is understated. Quality of haircut or hairstyle extremely important. Jewelry is limited to solid gold or platinum. Fit and quality of clothing and workmanship very important.

* Increasingly, two years of college is becoming a requirement for many occupations.

Some Key Hidden Rules to Understand in Transition from Beginning Supervision to Mid-Management

Once a person has gotten in on the ground floor, beginning

supervision is the first rung of the ladder. The key issue here is the ability

to motivate and work with individuals who are to be supervised without having the authority to hire and fire. Crucial to moving up the company ladder is the ability to work with people while you supervise them.

Very little training is provided at this level because usually it's done informally. Even when there are title changes and salary increases, for legal reasons supervisory responsibilities often aren't clearly identified. But the verbal expectation is that the monitoring of tasks and group task facilitation will take place.

Some of the more common mistakes by beginning supervisors are:

- The approach becomes overly directive (thereby offending co-workers).

- The supervisor is hesitant to state clearly what is to be done.

- Group jealousy becomes an issue; a we/they mentality develops.

- Resistance to the supervisor is too difficult to deal with, so he/she attempts to do most of the work on his/her own instead of delegating.

Training that addresses the above issues helps bring tools to the beginning supervisor.

Some Key Hidden Rules to Understand in Transition from Mid-Management to Executive Level

If you wish to be promoted to the executive level, please note some of the key mistakes that people often make.

When one is negotiating at the executive level, the question asked is this: Who is the best? Who has the most expertise? *Not* who is the least expensive. There is a clear understanding that you have to pay for expertise. The price is not negotiated up front but comes as a part of the working relationship. If you negotiate the price first, often the person with expertise will simply turn down the work, unless there is a compelling reason for him/her to accept it (usually it has to do with his/her own agenda). As a rule of thumb, people who are really good at what they do are very busy. Second, individuals with expertise are not interested in having their time wasted. So your respect for their time will be a key factor in developing a positive working relationship.

Another key aspect of the ability to move to the executive level is the network of connections that is established as one moves up from mid-management. A network of connections is absolutely vital to success at the executive level. How does one establish such connections? For individuals who don't have many connections, one of the first places to start is professional organizations at local, state, and national levels. These networks also can be established in political organizations.

In the process of developing networks of connections, membership in private clubs and organizations also is established. Sometimes these memberships are by invitation and sometimes by recommendation. It's important to note that hidden rules apply in these situations as well. When you're at the club, it's expected that you will *not* (a) abuse the relationships, (b) use a hard sell or push sales of your product/service, or (c) ask questions of a pointed nature about another member's business.

Networking is the lifeblood of the higher levels of corporate management. However ...

You Know Your Connections Are on Life Support When:

- You are socially excluded from invitations.
- Phone calls aren't returned.
- Key individuals won't lunch with you alone.
- You are excluded from key decision-making meetings.
- A position is created between you and your boss.

Why Are Connections Crucial?

Connections are crucial for several reasons. A reason often cited is that connections help you get promoted. And that is true. But the most important reason is the accuracy of information that connections allow you to have. Excellent connections enable you to locate the expertise needed to make sound decisions, and they also provide information that sometimes cannot be acknowledged in an open, written format.

For example, Antwaan wanted to buy a company in Saudi Arabia. He sensed that the information he was getting about the company was incomplete. Because of his long association with international professional organizations, he contacted a Saudi member of a professional group with whom he had developed a good relationship. Antwaan got the missing information he needed to make his decision.

A second example: Melissa was a rising star in mid-management. Officials with another company came to her and offered her a 35% raise to work for them. Through her connections, she found out that the woman who would be her boss had gone through four people in that position in two years. She declined the offer.

What Does This Mean?

First of all, a person won't necessarily be able to immediately know the requirements of the level into which he/she is moving. The real issue is whether or not he/she can learn – or is willing to learn – to meet those requirements.

Does this mean that one set of hidden rules is better than another? Absolutely not. It simply means that if one wishes to be promoted or operate within a context different from one's present situation, one needs to understand that there are different rules.

RUBRIC EXPLANATION

0   Knows and uses hidden rules of street at work.

Extreme example: A field-service hand of an oil company came into the main office and was flirting with one of the secretaries. He was telling her about the "f---ing" work, how "f---ing" hard it was, and what a "s---head" the boss was. The secretary said to him, "I don't appreciate your language; I find it offensive." The man looked at her in total surprise, then looked at another secretary and asked, "What the f--- did I *say?*"

1   Knows and uses hidden rules of hourly wages at work.

When an employee is being paid hourly wages, the work often is simply a way to make money. Work would never be taken home. Work is done at work and, if it can't be done within the allotted hours, then overtime will be paid.

2   Knows and uses hidden rules that members of mid-management follow at work.

The employee understands that when one is on salary at the mid-management level the job can't be done within the 40-hour workweek. There is an expectation of personal initiative both in getting the work done and in problem-solving.

3   Knows and uses hidden rules that officials at executive level follow at work. Knows hidden rules of country club.

At this level there is often a tendency to use people to get where the individual wants to go. And that will work for a while. But unless this person begins to think of connections as mutually beneficial, as opposed to being just for his/her own personal or professional gain, he/she likely won't get to Level 4.

4   Knows and uses hidden rules that are followed in corporate boardroom and with charities. Understands organizational, social, and business pedigree and hierarchy.

At this level the individual is operating with the end in mind. Furthermore, he/she is very careful to observe the protocols that are in effect in such matters as seating, serving, and communication patterns (e.g., who is expected to initiate the conversation, who must be introduced before the individual is acknowledged, who determines the seating patterns, who is seated next to whom, who is responsible for which introductions).

In addition, the power structures in the boardroom are known (who has the political leverage to change the decisions, who has the expertise that is readily acknowledged, who is respected, whose spouse carries such clout that he/she is making the decisions even though not physically in the room).

At this level the interplay between charities and causes is as integrally linked as is the interplay between politics and business. So to know the preferred charities, as well as the political connections of those in power, becomes crucial to long-term success.

HOW CAN I USE THIS INFORMATION?

If you have an employee whom you would like to promote, you can …	~ identify informally the hidden rules the employees knows and the ones he/she needs to learn. ~ teach the rules the individual needs to learn. ~ teach the hidden rules of your workplace to employees as part of their orientation.
If you suspect that you aren't being promoted because of hidden rules, you can …	~ find a mentor who will tell you stories about his/her position (often individuals cannot articulate outright the hidden rules they are using; stories are where the hidden rules emerge more clearly). ~ ask point-blank what you need to do to be promoted.
If you aren't sure whether the issues in a situation center on the cognitive, emotional, or hidden rules, you can say …	~ "Help me understand what you were thinking when _____ …"

WHAT DID THE RESEARCH FIND?

Our research revealed a very high correlation between hidden rules, job title, the amount of training received by the individual, and income. While the knowledge of hidden rules didn't have much effect on several of the other resources, it tremendously impacted income and job title. The correlation between job title, income, and hidden rules was .0002.

CHAPTER

4

YOU

DON'T

KNOW

ME

INTEGRITY
AND TRUST

	0	1	2	3	4
Integrity	Predictably amoral. Destructive to others. Practices deception.	Inconsistent. Unpredictable. No internal compass. Right and wrong are gray areas.	Consistently moral, ethical, and legal. Decides in best interests of self. Rationalizes poor decisions.	Decisions are moral, ethical, and legal. Avoids difficult issues. Is responsible for self but blames others.	Decisions are moral, ethical, and legal. Tough issues are addressed. Accepts responsibility for self and is accountable to others.

Integrity and Trust

Trust is linked to two issues – predictability and safety. In other words, can I know with some certainty that this person will do what he/she says? Can I predict with some accuracy that it will occur every time? The second part of the equation is safety: Will I be safe with this person?

Integrity is the extent to which there is congruence between actions and a moral/ethical code. Of note are two issues: the difference between being liked and being respected, and the issue of the organization vs. the individual. In his book *The Spirit to Serve Marriott's Way,* the authors state, "The organization is more important than the individual." Organizations are amoral by their very nature, so the individuals within the organization determine the extent to which the activities of the organization are moral and ethical.

Integrity is a huge issue in supervision. Crucial to the success of any business is getting accurate information, maintaining the legalities governing that business, and keeping track of the money. To have an employee who is dishonest is a serious liability for any business.

Further, at the executive level, it's paramount that the individual be more concerned about being respected than liked. The tough decisions are not easy. Few employees applaud the boss for tough decisions. Tough decisions *always* impact someone negatively in some fashion. What gives some people the edge is that they can hand out the tough decisions in a way that causes the least amount of pain.

Class Issues

It isn't unusual for an individual from poverty to have an innate distrust of corporations. The "system" is viewed as oppressive, and anyone who dances to the "company tune" is not to be trusted. There is little or no understanding of the reasons that structure exists within a company. It isn't unusual for a person raised in poverty to turn down a promotion to mid-management because such a role tends to be viewed skeptically as a form of disloyalty or even dishonesty. If one takes the new position, there's a fear that one will no longer be able to voice his/her true thoughts. There also may be the fear that more pressure will come with the new job and "who needs all that pressure?"

In the middle-class mindset, the moral, legal, and ethical codes must be followed. There are gray areas that can be manipulated, however.

In the wealth mindset, you make the laws and codes. You intervene at the policy-making level (court, legislatures, etc.) to make the ethical and legal codes what you wish them to be.

If an individual has a 0 or 1 in integrity, he/she should not be hired. If the individual has a 2 in integrity, he/she will need a great deal of supervision. Only if the individual has a 3 or 4 in integrity, should he/she be advanced.

It should be noted that in *all* classes personal integrity – i.e., you keep your word – is *extremely important.*

RUBRIC EXPLANATION

0   **Predictably amoral. Destructive to others. Practices deception.**

Fred works in a mobile home factory and is responsible for the mobile homes leaving the plant for their points of sale. The truckers who pick them up are given extra tires if they bring him a gift of some sort, such as steaks or a case of beer. The controller of the company, who *knows* about Fred's practice, calls Fred and tells him to keep a running inventory of tires so that the factory won't run out. The owner of the company likes Fred because Fred keeps the salesmen from selling the same mobile home twice. The owner doesn't have a computerized inventory system, and the owner himself cheats on his taxes. Fred helps the owner keep the internal theft reduced.

1   Inconsistent. Unpredictable. No internal compass. Right and wrong are gray areas.

Jason is a plant manager who also has a landscaping business of his own. During the day, he works as a plant manager but spends nearly half of his time on the phone managing his landscaping business. He uses equipment from the plant to help with his landscaping, but he always returns it. Yet he fires one of his landscaping employees because the guy borrowed a gas can from the plant to help a friend who had run out of gas.

2   Consistently moral, ethical, and legal. Decides in best interests of self. Rationalizes poor decisions.

Harry is a company's director of Human Resources and has a salary of $120,000 a year, plus benefits. Harry loves to be in the limelight. In his personal life, he's often late with his payments. When asking the bank vice president for an extension on his mortgage, he says, "It's so hard to be in my position. Everyone expects things from me, and I need to provide them. I had to go to the baseball playoffs. It's just expected."

3   Decisions are moral, ethical, and legal. Avoids difficult issues. Is responsible for self but blames others.

Jerry is an accountant with a small company. He is absolutely honest about money. However, when pressed with a personnel decision, he makes one that keeps the employees liking him. When the head of Receivables asks for an extension of her one-week vacation, Jerry says yes, even though there are several areas of responsibility she hasn't trained anyone to handle. So for that week the company is highly vulnerable because Jerry couldn't tell the employee no.

4   Decisions are moral, ethical, and legal. Tough issues are addressed. Accepts responsibility for self and is accountable to others.

A small company with a huge loss of revenues needs to cut four positions. A friend of the CEO holds one of the positions that has to go. The CEO cuts the position, even though it costs him the friendship.

Note: If an individual doesn't have at least a 2 in integrity, he/she is going to create many headaches for you. Typically companies don't provide training in ethics, but in reality, when ethics and integrity are made part of the corporate culture, problems are significantly reduced.

In my (Ruby's) own company I have embedded integrity into our corporate culture in at least these ways: First, we have strict policies about software copying and use; these policies are monitored and enforced. Second, the director of Finance maintains strict accounting mechanisms, which are not only legal but also ethical. And third, we have quickly dismissed employees who *deliberately* distorted information about other employees through omissions and deletions of vital information.

HOW CAN I USE THIS INFORMATION?

When an employee who has supervisory responsibilities will not confront, you can …	~ provide training in negotiation and conflict management.
When an employee has integrity issues, you can …	~ provide training in the expected ethical behaviors of your corporation. ~ make corporate ethics a part of the evaluation. ~ identify in writing the ethical policies of the corporation – such as software copying, use, etc.
In order not to hire someone at a Level 1 or 2, you can …	~ make integrity part of the interviewing questions, i.e., "What would you do if …?"

WHAT DID THE RESEARCH FIND?

Our research revealed that if an individual had a high level of integrity (3 or 4), he/she also had a high level of emotional resources, a high level of relationships that were nurturing and supportive, and a strong desire to succeed.

Furthermore, our research indicated that there was a very high correlation between job title, integrity, and income.

CHAPTER
5

IT'S

ABOUT

THE

MONEY

FINANCIAL
RESOURCES

	0	1	2	3	4
Financial	Bills unpaid. Creditors calling.	Paycheck to paycheck. Bills paid late.	More income than bills. Some savings.	Building assets in home. Limited investments.	Has net worth other than home. Many investments.

Financial Resources

Obtaining financial resources is often a motivation for work. While a key factor is how much you make, the real issue is how much you keep – and what you do with what is kept. Being able to operate at level 3 or 4 of the resource quotient indicates that a person has the ability to plan and control impulsivity.

In the book *Rich Dad, Poor Dad*, authors Kiyosaki and Lechter describe class differences in thinking about money. To understand money, one needs to be familiar with four terms: income, expenses, assets, and liabilities. In poverty, money comes from a job and goes into one pocket as income and out the other pocket as expenses. In middle class, money comes from a job and goes into one pocket as income but out of the other pocket as a liability (which eventually becomes an asset – example: a mortgage), which is a type of expense. But in wealth, money is generated from assets (not a job), and liabilities are engaged in while using someone else's money.

When an employee must ask for advances on his/her paycheck, when debt-collection agencies call at work, when the electricity is turned off … all have an impact on the effectiveness of the worker.

To be promoted from the mid-management level to the executive level, it isn't enough to make budgets and stay within the budget. A much wider range of financial issues must be brought to the table.

RUBRIC EXPLANATION

0   Bills unpaid. Creditors calling.

One of the ways this may reveal itself is that it's almost impossible to reach the person by phone. Creditors will call at work. The employee avoids phone calls and always wants to know who's calling.

1   Paycheck to paycheck. Bills paid late.

A way this may become evident is when an employee frequently asks for an advance on his/her paycheck.

2   More income than bills. Some savings.

This employee has a rudimentary understanding of money management.

3   Building assets in home. Limited investments.

The idea of assets and liabilities is present. Some concepts of the

notion of investing – including the risks and liabilities that come with

investing – are understood.

4   Has net worth other than home. Many investments.

This individual has an understanding of assets and liabilities, cash

flow, and the risks of investing.

NOTE: A SIXTH LEVEL (WHICH ISN'T ON THE RESOURCE QUOTIENT) CONCERNING FINANCIAL RESOURCES COULD BE STATED AS FOLLOWS:

5   Has retainer for Certified Public Accountant and portfolio manager.

Has personal knowledge to analyze portfolio and holdings. Pays for

services of individuals who have expertise in strategic financial data.

Uses predictive and statistical data for financial decision-making.

Financial decision-making is made for generations to come. Has trust(s).

Level 5 is the level of understanding that must exist to effectively

operate at the executive level of a corporation. While the individual may

not personally have all the assets listed in 5, an understanding of those

assets must be present.

The reason this financial information becomes so important in the workplace is that the use of personal money indicates levels of integrity, self-discipline, and knowledge. The common thinking has been that personal money is unrelated to success in the workplace. That thinking is as erroneous as believing that drug use outside of the workplace doesn't affect the job site. As in anything else, it's the degree of disruption that impacts the workplace. But knowledge of both 4 and 5 is essential to achieving promotion to the executive level.

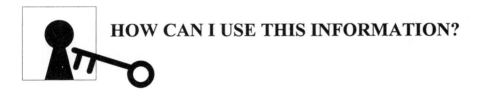 **HOW CAN I USE THIS INFORMATION?**

If you have an employee who is "welfare to workforce," you can ...	~ teach the "envelope" system of money.
If you have employees who are having financial problems, you can ...	~ refer them to the Web, to local services, or to "employee assistance."
To enhance the overall financial awareness of your employees whom you wish to promote, you can ...	~ teach them about financial concepts and corporate budgets. ~ ask the finance person or department to provide a one-hour overview. ~ mentor them about finances.
To increase the capabilities of your employees and therefore their own knowledge, you can ...	~ add tuition-paid college courses to the cafeteria plan of benefits. ~ reimburse for tuition.

* To increase your own chances of promotion, you can educate yourself by …	~ reading books and articles about finance. ~ subscribing to *The Wall Street Journal, Forbes, Business Week, Chronicle of Philanthropy,* etc. ~ going on-line and getting information. ~ lunching with knowledgeable people and asking them to teach you. ~ finding a mentor.

An understanding of corporate statements, budgets, assets, liabilities, etc., provides a considerable edge in both for-profit and not-for-profit organizations. To be ignorant regarding this topic is to invite disaster.

 # WHAT DID THE RESEARCH FIND?

Our research showed a strong correlation between a high financial score and the overall score on the resource quotient. In other words, if the individual had a higher (3 or 4) score on financial resources, the overall score on the resource quotient was much higher. We found that almost a precise correlation existed between the job title and financial resources.

CHAPTER

6

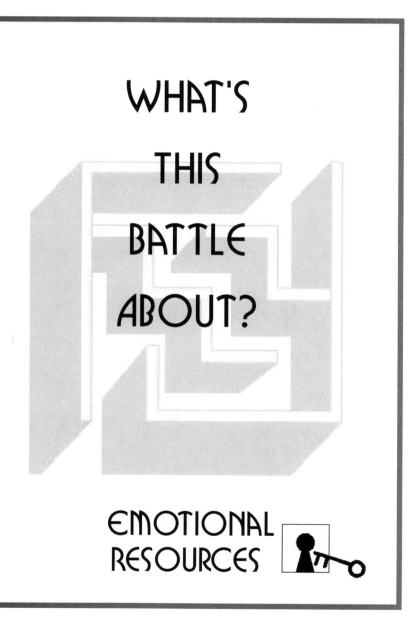

WHAT'S

THIS

BATTLE

ABOUT?

EMOTIONAL
RESOURCES

	0	1	2	3	4
Emotional	No emotional stamina. Impulsive. Engages in self-destructive behavior (addiction, violence, abusive adult relationships, casual sex).	Moves between voices of child and parent. Blames and accuses. Impulsive. Mood swings.	Uses adult voice except in conflict. Outbursts of anger. Sometimes engages in impulsive behavior.	Uses adult voice in conflict. Avoids conflict. Rarely impulsive.	Uses adult voice in conflict. Confronts, yet maintains relationships. Is not impulsive.

Emotional Resources

Two issues in particular influence the ability of an individual to deal with conflict in the workplace and in his/her personal life: One is the ability to listen, and the other is the ability to translate from the personal to the objective.

'He Don't Listen'

Six aspects of language affect the ability of a person to "listen" in the workplace: verbal/non-verbal, concrete to abstract, language registers, discourse patterns, story structure, and ability to formulate questions. To "listen" means that one has the ability to distinguish what is important from what is not; to ascertain what is *really* being said, i.e., what the issues are; and to identify the impact of the information, issues, and emotions on the person and the organization. "Listening" is more than hearing, and it's based partly on cognitive patterns learned in the environment.

In listening, what happens inside the head of the listener is crucial. The listener can choose to "sort" the information emotionally, cognitively, or neither. In other words, the information can be sorted and taken personally, it can be sorted against an issue, or it can be ignored. Inside the head, the sorting is done either by the purpose for listening or by the structure of the content. For example, if one is being told a joke, the sorting is for the humor. If one is watching a talk show, the sorting is for the personalities and/or the humor. But if one is in a new city and is listening to someone describe how to get to the public library, one is sorting for sequence and direction. The mind sorts information as it listens. When a person listens or remembers, he/she has sorted for particular information.

Verbal/Non-Verbal

In poverty, the most important information tends to be conveyed *non*-verbally. In most workplaces and in the professional corporation, there's a tendency toward much greater reliance on words to communicate the vital information. Martin Joos, a Dutch linguist, did a study on languages. He found that no matter what language one speaks, there are five registers. These are presented in the following table.

Language Registers

REGISTER	EXPLANATION
Frozen	Language that is always the same. For example: Lord's Prayer, wedding vows, etc.
Formal	The standard sentence syntax and word choice of work and school. Has complete sentences and specific word choice.
Consultative	Formal register when used in conversation. Discourse pattern not quite as direct as formal register.
Casual	Language between friends and is characterized by a 400- to 800-word vocabulary. Word choice general and not specific. Conversation dependent upon non-verbal assists. Sentence syntax often incomplete.
Intimate	Language between lovers or twins. Language of sexual harassment.

Research by Anita Hart (1995) and Maria Rosario Montano-Harmon (1991) indicates that the primary language register known and used in poverty is casual register. It has about half the words of formal register and contains few abstract words. In fact, Hart found in her research that a 3-year-old in a professional household has a more extensive vocabulary than an adult in a welfare household! So if an individual has only casual register, he/she is sorting for the non-verbal first, then the words.

Concrete to Abstract

Because casual register has so few abstract words, many arguments and much communication in the workplace quickly turn personal. If people have a limited number of abstract words, they don't have the cognitive capability of resolving arguments because they can't go to the issue level. One of the characteristics of individuals who do get promoted is that they have the ability to resolve conflicts and/or lessen conflict levels. To do so, emotional and personal episodes must be translated to the issue level, which involves abstractions. For example, I once heard a husband and wife argue for 15 minutes about which one the cat loved most. They were really arguing about who was most lovable. Instead of dealing with the issue, the argument became personal. The ability to listen for the issue, so that it can be resolved at a non-personal level, is pivotal for promotion.

Discourse Patterns

Communication is further complicated by discourse patterns. The discourse of a discussion is the meat, the logic, of it. In formal register the expectation is that the person will get right to the point. But in casual register you go around the mulberry bush a few times to determine your feelings based on the non-verbals in a situation. If the boss expects a get-to-the-point type of approach, and the employee is always beating around the bush, chances are high that the promotion will be denied, simply because of the amount of time it takes to deal with the person and the difficulty in obtaining vital data.

FORMAL-REGISTER DISCOURSE PATTERN

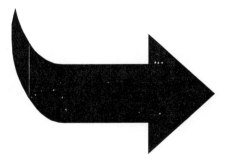

SPEAKER OR WRITER GETS STRAIGHT TO THE POINT.

CASUAL-REGISTER DISCOURSE PATTERN

WRITER OR SPEAKER GOES AROUND THE ISSUE BEFORE FINALLY COMING TO THE POINT.

Story Structure

Furthermore, the structure of a story is different, depending on the use of casual or formal register. In formal register, a story is told from the beginning to the end, with cause, effect, and sequence by time. The story revolves around a plot – what happened. In casual register (this is what is used in gossip), one starts at the end first. Then episodes or vignettes are shared, along with spontaneous comments from the listeners. This is the principal story structure of TV sitcoms. It's also the story structure preferred in poverty.

STORY STRUCTURE

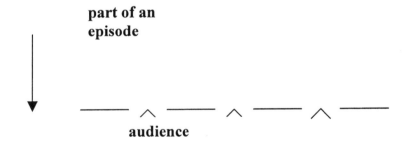

B   PLOT   E

THE FORMAL-REGISTER STORY STRUCTURE STARTS AT THE BEGINNING OF THE STORY AND GOES TO THE END IN A CHRONOLOGICAL OR ACCEPTED NARRATIVE PATTERN. THE MOST IMPORTANT PART OF THE STORY IS THE PLOT.

part of an episode

audience

THE CASUAL-REGISTER STORY STRUCTURE BEGINS WITH THE END OF THE STORY FIRST OR THE PART WITH THE GREATEST EMOTIONAL INTENSITY. THE STORY IS TOLD IN VIGNETTES, WITH AUDIENCE PARTICIPATION THROUGHOUT. THE STORY ENDS WITH A COMMENT ABOUT THE CHARACTER AND HIS/HER VALUE. THE MOST IMPORTANT PART OF THE STORY IS THE CHARACTERIZATION.

In other words, if an employee constantly uses the episodic story structure, the boss often doesn't want to advance that person because of the time and trouble involved in getting pertinent information. Cause and effect revolve around time sequence; being able to resolve a problem or issue requires the identification of cause and effect.

Ability to Formulate Questions

Listening is augmented by the ability to invert the order of words to create a question. Many adults are unable to do this. Instead, they make a statement and non-verbally turn it into a question. For example, "You don't have any more?" That is a statement that has been non-verbally made into a question. A true question would be "Don't you have any more?" When an individual cannot ask a question syntactically, he/she has difficulty resolving an issue. The main option in such a case is simply making comments. At that point the person with the problem goes away saying, "He don't listen."

Three Additional Factors That Create Conflict

Three additional issues influence the level of conflict in the workplace: voices, "win/lose," and triangling. Promotions generally aren't given to individuals who create a great deal of conflict, unless an individual is brought in specifically as a change agent. The amount of energy and time taken away from the corporation in conflict is extremely expensive. The ability to avoid – or at least minimize – conflict is crucial to promotion.

To be promoted to mid-management, one must be able to use formal register and the adult voice in conflict, listen to the non-verbals, and avoid triangling. In addition, it's vital for the individual to use the formal discourse pattern.

Voices

One of the greatest conflict-makers and conflict-reducers is the use of voices. Eric Berne did a great deal of work in the early 1960s with the concept of voices. Basically, each of us has three personas or voices that we use internally and externally to communicate – a child voice, a parent voice, and an adult voice.

CHILD

- ~ *Quit picking on me.*
- ~ *You don't love me.*
- ~ *You want me to leave.*
- ~ *Nobody likes (loves) me.*
- ~ *I hate you.*
- ~ *You're ugly.*
- ~ *You make me sick.*
- ~ *It's your fault.*
- ~ *Don't blame me.*
- ~ *She, he, _____ did it.*
- ~ *You make me mad.*
- ~ *You made me do it.*

PARENT

- ~ *You shouldn't (should) do that.*
- ~ *It's wrong (right) to do _____.*
- ~ *That's stupid, immature, out of line, ridiculous.*
- ~ *Life's not fair. Get busy.*
- ~ *You are good, bad, worthless, beautiful (any judgmental, evaluative comment).*
- ~ *You do as I say.*
- ~ *If you weren't so _____, this wouldn't happen to you.*
- ~ *Why can't you be like _____?*

ADULT

- ~ *I need ...*
- ~ *What's your plan?*
- ~ *What are the choices in this situation?*
- ~ *If you choose _____, then you have chosen _____.*
- ~ *If you did know, what would you say?*
- ~ *When you did that, what did you want?*
- ~ *How did that behavior help you be successful?*

The Child Voice

When a boss or supervisor speaks to an employee in a child voice (whines), this indicates that manipulation and favoritism are the norm, that issues are not identified clearly, and that the structures and guidelines of the organization are not being followed.

The Parent Voice

There's a parent voice that is positive, supportive, and insistent. But the parent voice that is negative and judgmental (such an individual often speaks with his/her index finger in the air) disrupts the work environment and causes many employees to quit – or want to quit. It also ends up causing supervisors to expend a lot of energy dealing with latent hostility, a description that goes something like this: "I'll get even with you when you aren't looking." Latent hostility is a powder keg waiting for a spark. Bosses who depend on the negative parent voice have a high turnover rate, frequent crises, and numerous complaints.

The Adult Voice

To use the adult voice, however, one must have the ability to formulate questions (explained earlier in this chapter). The supervisor who uses the adult voice consistently has fewer conflicts and less hostility. The adult voice allows issues to be resolved. It also places responsibility where it belongs – on the shoulders of the person who caused the problem.

Win/Lose

Individuals who rely heavily on the negative parent voice often create a win/lose situation; power struggles are an almost inevitable byproduct of the negative parent voice. Further, such individuals often engage in verbal abuse, which exacerbates any pre-existing latent hostility in an organization. What is verbal abuse? It's when the intent of the message sender is to hurt, demean, or humiliate the message receiver.

The person who is able to stay in the adult voice reduces conflict, gets issues resolved, and often gets promoted.

Triangling

This is the classic "He said, she said, they said" situation. Triangling almost always involves an instigator and tends to be much more prevalent when the boss either relies on the child voice or the negative parent voice. The amount of time and energy that "He said, she said, they said" can devour in an organization can be astronomical.

Triangling is the pattern in which two people or groups will side with or against another individual or group. The less stable a situation is politically – or the scarcer the resources are in an organization – the greater the amount of triangling. In politically charged situations, the landscape changes frequently as to which individuals or groups are siding with or against each other.

Triangling limits the effectiveness of the individual, the department, and the corporation. The basic structure is that Person A is mad at, or has been hurt by, Person B. Instead of talking to Person B to clear up the issue between them, Person A talks to Person C about the situation. Sometimes Person A wants empathy and understanding. Sometimes, though, Person A is intent upon a power play to coerce or sabotage Person B into compliance. In either case, Person C tells Person A what he/she wants to hear or else gives advice that isn't particularly helpful. Then Person C goes to Person B and tells him/her what Person A said. And so it goes … on and on. Typically, such triangling causes other people also to get involved, expanding the morass and sucking more and more victims into the swamp.

By not taking part in triangling, an individual avoids both unproductive time and the creation of enemies. He/she, then, often is recommended and chosen for promotion because of a healthier pattern of interpersonal communication (in other words, more straightforward interaction, less gossip). Phrases that can be used to avoid triangling are:

- "I would be glad to discuss it if both of you are in the room."

- "Were you there when that was said?"

- "How does that affect your ability to do your work?"

- "What processes or procedures could we put into place to keep that from happening again in the future?"

- "What tasks do you need to devote time to at this moment?"

RUBRIC EXPLANATION

0   No emotional stamina. Impulsive. Engages in self-destructive behavior (addiction, violence, abusive adult relationships, casual sex).

When emotional stamina is present, the individual who's alone is fine. When there's no emotional stamina, the individual almost always needs people around. This is the employee who divulges inappropriate information in return for a favor – or is out all night at the trade show and unable to function well the next day. Self-destructive behavior almost always shows up eventually in the workplace.

1   Moves between voices of child and parent. Blames and accuses. Impulsive. Mood swings.

This employee creates difficulties in the workplace because of a lack of predictability and the inability to take personal responsibility for his/her actions. Furthermore, problems are invariably someone else's fault. In an argument, the language is "you this" and "you that ..."

2   Uses adult voice except in conflict. Outbursts of anger. Sometimes engages in impulsive behavior.

This individual takes personal responsibility for his/her actions but has difficulty with conflict and the articulation of feelings. So the employee often lets an issue "fester" until he/she explodes. Because of this inability to articulate feelings, impulsiveness will surface periodically. This worker may create financial liabilities for the company because of inappropriate ways in which confrontations are handled.

To illustrate: Lance was a line foreman. One of his crew, Curt, was constantly late and often flirting with the boss's daughter who was a receptionist for the company. One day Curt was late again and cost his crew a production bonus. In front of everyone Lance yelled at him and said, "You crazy _____ (ethnic/cultural slur) moron!" After word of the incident got back to the boss, Lance lost his job.

3 Uses adult voice in conflict. Avoids conflict. Rarely impulsive.

These individuals take personal responsibility and usually can deal with conflict. But they dislike conflict, thereby avoiding confrontation. They attempt to manipulate the situation from behind the scenes. These employees often end up creating costs for the company in personnel. They frequently hire additional staff (if possible) rather than confront the existing staff members about inappropriate activities. These individuals have difficulty sorting out personal from objective issues.

4 Uses adult voice in conflict. Confronts, yet maintains relationships. Is not impulsive.

These individuals have the ability to articulate issues in a non-offensive way and can sort out the personal from the objective. They can address the issues, develop a plan, and often (though not always) keep the relationship intact. Conflicts are dealt with initially by asking lots of questions, rather than by making statements.

HOW CAN I USE THIS INFORMATION?

If you have an employee who cannot resolve conflicts, you can …	~ teach and require a process that includes the following:
	    a. What is the issue?
	    b. What happened (cause and effect)?
	    c. What is important emotionally?
	    d. What process or solution do we put into place so that it doesn't happen again?
	[Put the "adult voice" phrases of page 99 on your desk or by your phone, then use them.]

If you have an employee who uses only casual register, you can …	~ provide the phrases he/she needs to do a task. ~ have him/her teach the task to someone else, using those phrases.
If you wish to minimize group conflicts, you can …	~ teach the three voices to a group, then refer to the concept of voices rather than address the matter at the personal level.

WHAT DID THE RESEARCH FIND?

Our research revealed that a high correlation existed between emotional resources and integrity, i.e., if an individual had a high score in integrity, he/she also had a high score in emotional resources. In other words, the ability to control impulsivity and the ability to deal with conflict in a constructive way was directly linked to a high score in integrity.

CHAPTER
7

IT'S
NOT
NECESSARILY
ABOUT
INTELLIGENCE

MENTAL
RESOURCES

Mental	Relies totally on casual register and non-verbal data to communicate. Not much formal education. Disorganized.	Can read and write formal register. Prefers casual register. Can do basic math. Has difficulty managing time and tasks.	Knows when to use formal register. Has some training beyond high school. Can implement a plan if told how. Knows the <u>what</u> but not the <u>how</u>.	Uses formal register well. Formal education. Can do long-range planning. Knows the <u>what</u> and the <u>how</u>.	Consistently uses formal register well. Knows the <u>what</u> and the <u>why</u>. Initiates and executes plans. Congruence between non-verbals and words.

Mental Resources

As was stated in Chapter Five, a key piece in functioning and communicating in the workplace is the ability to move from the concrete (i.e., sensory/feeling base) to the abstract (i.e., using representational systems). Formal schooling is largely about the acquisition and use of abstract representational systems. Intellectual capital is the ability to manipulate those abstract representational systems.

In order to manipulate an abstract representational system, one must move to a mental model. What is a mental model? It can be a story, an analogy, or a two-dimensional drawing. For example, when someone is building a house, there's a lot of talk, which tends to be abstract and representational. But when the house is finally ready to be built in three dimensions, blueprints are almost always used. The blueprint is the mental model, the two-dimensional representation of the abstract talk. To read a blueprint is to be able to use a representational system. To be sure, the person with the most impressive intellectual capital is the one who can *create* the blueprint.

Why is intelligence not necessarily a significant factor in the ability to create or manipulate a mental model? Psychologist Jerome Bruner states that all intelligence is a function of both task and context. In the field of cognition and neuroscience, an understanding is emerging, namely: About half of what makes up a human being is determined by heredity and about half by environment. The point? Survival in poverty requires a very concrete, non-verbal approach to life, whereas survival in the world of work increasingly requires highly abstract, verbal capabilities.

In order to negotiate the work world, an abstract representational system inside the head is needed to replicate the external reality.

Replicating external reality is evidenced in these activities: planning (using abstract measures of time, space, and "part to whole" to do so), controlling impulsivity, sorting systematically through data using patterns, formulating questions (can invert word order to make questions; this was covered in Chapter Five), planning and labeling tasks (having both a plan and vocabulary for the task).

Planning

What does all this mean at work? For starters, planning requires a mental model for time, space, and "part to whole." In planning, the procedural steps are important. Where will you start? If you can't plan well, you don't know where to begin.

Time

The individual must have an abstract notion of time. Reuven Feuerstein found that most people tend to keep time emotionally, not abstractly. In other words, time is kept on the basis of how it feels, not on the basis of minutes and hours. A mental model for time that includes a past, present, and future is necessary. In poverty, time is often only the present: survival.

Additionally, the ability to abstractly estimate the amount of time a task will take is not developed. Therefore, the work often doesn't get done because the judgment about the amount of time the task would take was inaccurate.

What can one do to develop better habits with respect to time?

Teach employees to plan backward. In other words, draw a simple grid for a task.

Monday	Tuesday	Wednesday	Thursday	Friday

If a task is due on Friday, go to the space marked "Friday" and write, "Task is to be finished." Then say, "What do you have to do on Tuesday, Wednesday, and Thursday, so that it will be done on Friday?" In *The Seven Habits of Highly Effective People,* Stephen Covey says, "Begin with the end in mind." In other words, break down the tasks into parts and then ask, "How much time will you need each day to get this done?"

For adults from poverty, the workday is often interrupted by personal demands. A relative who just landed in jail might call, or someone's car broke down. A clear understanding needs to be established among employees that work time belongs to work. Just as they don't come into work on their personal time, they don't do personal things on their work time. Or at least they draw clear boundaries and keep personal matters to a minimum.

Space

To do math, read a map, put things together, and follow directions, an individual must have an orientation in space – i.e., north, south, east, west, left, right, up, down.

The human body operates in space. One way to keep track of space is through touch or concreteness. Another way is through direction and abstract spatial references. Because math is about assigning order and value to the universe, we tend to do it via direction – i.e., we write small to large numbers from left to right or top to bottom.

For adults who don't have a clear orientation in space, one way to teach it is to create a two-dimensional drawing/map and teach them to turn the map with their body until they have the ability to turn it inside their head.

'Part to Whole'

The workplace requires individuals to have the notion of "part to whole" and "whole to part." Again, one of the easiest ways to teach this is to list the parts of the task or to make a drawing of all the parts, identifying each part.

Controlling Impulsivity

Poor impulse control exhibits itself when tasks are rushed through, projects are abandoned for another activity, budgets aren't followed, etc. One of the best ways to address this with adults is to teach goal-setting. Goal-setting must be done in writing, or it has little power. It can be as simple as having the employees write down their goals for that day. At the end of the day, they check to see if those goals were met.

Planning is the key to finishing tasks and controlling impulsivity. Even more importantly, according to brain research, the primary filter for what gets noticed by the mind is what the goals are. So when there is no planning, there are no goals. Related here is the ancient adage, "Where there is no vision, the people perish." When there's no planning, then simple emotional need or association determines one's activities.

Sorting Using Patterns

Brain research also reveals that few details are remembered over time, but patterns are. Therefore, learning can be enhanced if the patterns are directly taught – particularly to individuals who have no prior knowledge of the patterns.

When patterns are known, sorting through information or tasks becomes much faster and more efficient. In problem-solving, it becomes important to be able to sort through a great deal of information. Solutions can be generated or dismissed faster based on the patterns involved.

A study done with people who work in blue-collar technical fields (such as air-conditioning and plumbing) found that information about patterns is often passed on in stories. For example: "This case is just like the problem we had at the Sutter house."

Planning and Labeling Tasks

Another aspect of planning is the completion of tasks. To complete tasks, labels (vocabulary) and procedures must be assigned. One of the biggest problems for individuals at work is the number of items or portions of a task that simply are not addressed because a systematic method isn't used. We recommend four systems that can be used to systematically address a task: numbering, lettering, color-coding, and symbols/icons.

Creating Mental Models of Vocations or Disciplines

Further, to be an excellent employee, one must know the structure of that area of work or discipline. Each vocation and subject has specific ways of coding and keeping its knowledge. If a worker knows these, it's much easier to access the pertinent information necessary for decision making.

Having such a knowledge base is becoming an increasingly vital issue in workplaces – for two reasons: (1) As employers begin to use cross-discipline teams, team members often think very differently because they use the structure of their discipline/vocation to order their own thinking processes. So communication becomes a big issue. (2) Without understanding the mental models of the discipline, workers don't know what's important and what isn't, nor do they know what can be successfully manipulated/changed and what can't.

A strong suggestion would be to start from two-dimensional drawings rather than words when working with cross-discipline teams, new concepts, and new-employee orientations. Simple worksheets that have one column for *how* (the process) and one column for *why* (the concept) greatly speed up the learning process.

RUBRIC EXPLANATION

0   Relies totally on casual register and non-verbal data to communicate. Not much formal education. Disorganized.

This worker will say things like "I ain't got none." A corporation I worked with hired individuals at Level 1 and Level 2 to answer the phone to take airline reservations. A script was given to the employees to use for dealing with clients. The script was in formal register. On several occasions, the employee would become rattled by the customer making the reservation and get "off script." Flustered, the employee would revert to casual register and say things like, "You can kiss my ass." This didn't help sell tickets.

1   Can read and write formal register. Prefers casual register. Can do basic math. Has difficulty managing time and tasks.

This individual has formal register but doesn't have many of the mental models necessary for success in the workplace – namely models for time and space. Consequently, jobs don't get finished on time, correspondence is less than logical, filing systems are nonexistent (the person often can't find anything), and some tasks are never finished.

Following is a letter that one of Ruby's former employees (from a temporary agency) wrote; it was intercepted and didn't go out. Because of a flooding situation that had recently occurred, some participants were

unable to attend a training workshop. (Editor's note: All errors in the

ensuing letter have been intentionally retained.)

Let me begin to inform you that we cannot express our concern for your absence in the June Training of the Trainers. We understand that the difficulties that were involved in arriving were too great for some participants enrolled in this workshop. If at all possible we would have spoken with everyone to ensure a route to get there safely, but in this matter that was impossible; our apologies go out to you.

This matter has forced our company to allow options for your inconvenience. Unfortunately we are not going to be able to grant permission for refunds of any type. Reason begin that we were still able to hold the workshop without any difficulties and over 180 people were able to attend the workshop without any problem. Needless to say we are not trying to state in any way that you were, indeed, not able to participate in the workshop because of some type of catastrophe. There are many reasons why an individual could not have attended the workshop, but on the same note if our office were to go and identify and handle each situation differently than we would be handling this for days maybe weeks. Not to say that you are not worth are time, because you are. The options that we are offering are fair and quite manageable to everyone who unfortunately could not attend this workshop.

Option 1 is going to be attending the workshop that we have coming up in October. Option 2 is going to be attending the workshop we have coming up in December. Payment can be transferred in full to either workshop because of the circumstances that lie. When you make your decision, please call _____ and speak to _____ and I will get you all squared up as you need to be. If the options are not what you would consider fair, than please feel free to call and express your case at the same above number and speak, once again, to me and we will see what we can do for your situation. Thank you very much and I'll be waiting to here back from you.

Notice the circular discourse pattern, the incorrect usage of formal register, the homophone errors (missed by Spell-Check), and the mix of formal and casual – e.g., we'll "get you all squared up." In addition, the writer clearly had great difficulty sorting what was and wasn't important.

2   Knows when to use formal register. Has some training beyond high school. Can implement a plan if told how. Knows the <u>what</u> but not the <u>how</u>.

This person doesn't have difficulty with formal register or discourse pattern. He/she can get to the point. But the issues have to do with planning, the mental models of the occupation, and issues around time. Typically if an individual can't plan, he/she often doesn't have sequential procedural knowledge or the ability to manage time. He/she can tell you what needs to be done but often doesn't get it done.

3   Uses formal register well. Formal education. Can do long-range planning. Knows the <u>what</u> *and* the <u>how</u>.

These employees will do everything you tell them to do … and do it well. But they won't initiate much on their own. Their work is typically excellent. But they generally don't have an understanding of the mental models that govern their occupation or company. Nor do they have strategic knowledge about a company's abstract internal infrastructure –

or about the abstract external architectures a company needs to build in order to survive.

4   Consistently uses formal register well. Knows the <u>what</u> and the <u>why</u>. Initiates and executes plans. Congruence between non-verbals and words.

This individual brings to the workplace an understanding of what the corporation must do to develop growth. He/she not only can analyze but also can build abstract architectures through the implementation of processes, knows how to strategically place his/her division in the larger context, and can devise strategic plans to address market share.

central massachusetts center for

healthycommunities

A Program of LUK, Inc.
Funded by the MA Dept. of Public Health
44 Front Street, Suite 280
Worcester, MA 01608-1733
www.cmchc.org

HOW CAN I USE THIS INFORMATION?

If you have an employee who is disorganized, you can …	~ give him/her a numbering system or a color-coding system for the organization. ~ have him/her make a two-dimensional drawing of his/her space and where things are.
If you have an employee who doesn't get tasks finished and/or cannot plan, you can …	~ make a step sheet (the steps to complete the task and the approximate amount of time each task will take). ~ teach the employee to plan backward, i.e., "This is due on Friday, meaning such-and-such must be done on Thursday, Wednesday, etc." ~ teach the employee to prioritize tasks – what is most important, what can be left until later, etc.
If you have an employee who doesn't understand what is and isn't important, you can …	~ give him/her key questions to ask regarding the task/issues. ~ produce a copy of the company's mission statement and talk about it.
If you have an employee who doesn't understand the mental models of the company or his/her specific job, you can …	~ provide a story, analogy, or a 2-D drawing.
If you have an employee who doesn't understand key abstract concepts, you can …	~ provide the phrases the employee needs to use. ~ assign a facilitator to important discussions so that arguments are avoided. ~ change his/her work assignments. ~ provide mental models.

www.ahaprocess.com

 # WHAT DID THE RESEARCH FIND?

Our research showed a perfect correlation between mental resources and job title (.0000). A very high correlation existed between income and mental resources. Additionally, there was a high correlation between the individual's support system, the level of desire, and his/her mental resources. The development of the mind is a gift – both to oneself and to the company for which one works

CHAPTER

8

I THINK
I CAN,
I THINK
I CAN

SPIRITUAL
RESOURCES

	0	1	2	3	4
Spiritual destiny	Has no hope. Believes in fate. Choices and consequences are not linked. Discipline is about punishment, penance, and forgiveness.	Believes in good and bad luck. Few choices are considered. Tries not to get caught.	Believes that choices affect destiny. Options are examined. Choices and consequences are linked. Believes in a higher power.	Believes that choices affect destiny. Is affiliated with spiritual, religious, or humanitarian group. Is self-governing. Believes in a higher power.	Thoughts and choices determine destiny. Actively participates in and supports humanitarian causes. Believes in a higher power and purpose larger than self.

Spiritual Resources and Destiny

Psychologists refer to this as the internal and external locus of control. In other words, do you see yourself as having choices, or are you merely a victim of fate or circumstance? This is related to your beliefs about destiny. Such a resource is the belief in divine support and guidance, as well as the belief that an individual in many ways creates his/her own destiny. Spirituality brings hope and often resources from organized religion (but not always). An individual can have a strong spiritual orientation, yet not belong to any organized religious group.

In poverty, the belief system is often centered around fate and luck. As long as a situation can be blamed on luck or fate, there's little chance of change in behavior. Typical of this approach to life would be the comment, "That boy is bad to the bone." Discipline isn't about choices and consequences; rather it's about punishment, penance, and forgiveness.

On the other hand, the belief that to a large extent one controls what happens in one's life is a powerful resource.

RUBRIC EXPLANATION

0   Has no hope. Believes in fate. Choices and consequences are not linked. Discipline is about punishment, penance and forgiveness.

For these individuals, the system is against them, the boss doesn't like them, the world isn't fair. Their own role – and sense of possibility – in the situation is seldom if ever examined.

1   Believes in good and bad luck. Few choices are considered. Tries not to get caught.

This individual often buys lottery tickets. In fact, one of the most common items found in repossessed cars is an assortment of lottery tickets.

2   Believes that choices affect destiny. Options are examined. Choices and consequences are linked. Believes in a higher power.

This individual believes that life has a purpose and that there is hope. Life is about more than daily existence. There is an understanding that certain actions lead to certain consequences. This impacts the

workplace because individuals bring energy to work when that work is

linked to purpose and hope.

3   Believes that choices affect destiny. Is affiliated with spiritual, religious, or humanitarian group. Is self-governing. Believes in a higher power.

For this individual the concept of "giving back" exists. It isn't

enough to care for oneself. One also cares about and for others. This can

be an asset in the workplace because employees see themselves as part of

a larger group. The well-being of the larger group is considered in

choices made by the individual.

4   Thoughts and choices determine destiny. Actively participates in and supports humanitarian causes. Believes in a higher power and purpose larger than self.

This individual realizes that he/she can shape the future by making

choices and decisions that will impact that future.

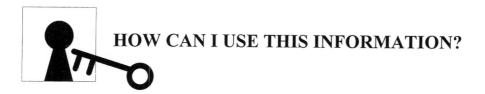

HOW CAN I USE THIS INFORMATION?

If you have an employee who believes he/she is fated, you can …	~ provide stories of people who had the "odds" stacked against them, yet were able to triumph over adversity.
	~ provide opportunities through your organization for community service.
	~ offer an hour a week (paid) in which the employee mentors someone (i.e., students through the local schools, Big Brothers/Big Sisters, etc.).
	~ talk about choices the worker made, along with alternative choices he/she could have made.
	~ engage the employee in long-term planning.

WHAT DID THE RESEARCH FIND?

Our research indicated that a high correlation existed between the individual's spiritual resources, the nature of his/her support system, and relationships that were nurturing and positive. An individual who has spiritual resources usually has a healthy support system and a strong set of relationships that are nurturing and positive.

CHAPTER

9

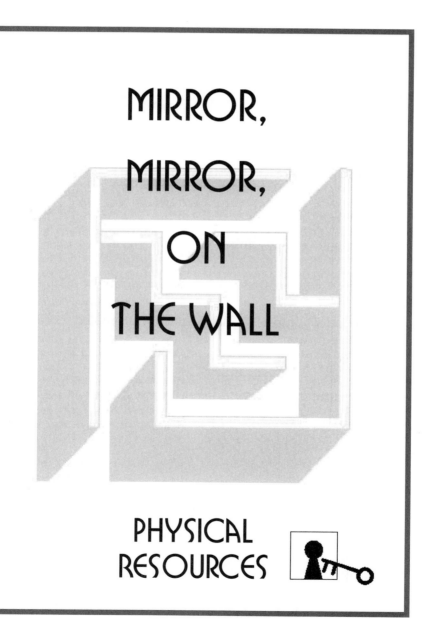

MIRROR,
MIRROR,
ON
THE WALL

PHYSICAL
RESOURCES

	0	1	2	3	4
Physical	Cannot take care of physical self. Requires assistance. Risky behaviors create health problems.	Can take care of self. Often sick. *Or* can take care of self but does not. Unkempt.	Clean, presentable. Able to take care of self. Mostly healthy.	Attractive. Physically able. Mostly healthy.	Very attractive. Weight, height proportional. Excellent physical health.

Physical Resources

Physical resources make a big difference in life. The ability to take care of yourself and do for yourself is of inestimable value. If I am bedridden, I not only cannot care for myself; I must have someone around me who can take care of me.

Moreover, research shows that physical appearance affects both hiring and promotion. Attractive individuals are promoted more often than unattractive ones. The weight, appearance, and overall fitness of an individual all contribute to perceptions that others have.

Clothing

Clothing becomes a subset of physical resources because it's part how one's physical resources appear to others.

John Molloy has done extensive research on the impact of clothing and appearance on promotion. His book *Dress for Success* identifies by occupation, position, and class the clothing that is acceptable and is not. Because appearance plays such a large role in hiring and promotion, a closer look is now given to it. Apparel also is one of the first indicators of an individual's social class.

In old money (two generations or more of wealth), clothing is often understated, but it is made of very high-quality materials. What one pays attention to is the fit and the quality of the clothes. For social events, the artistic merit of the clothing is also important. In purchasing expensive apparel, you're buying the fit and the quality of material and workmanship. Not much jewelry is worn in old money, but what is worn is of high quality and often "designer." Clothing tends to be in muted shades for daily wear; Molloy is very specific about the importance of this.

In new money (one generation of high income), the concept of fit and quality of workmanship is often misunderstood. Jewelry frequently is overstated, even garish.

In middle class, clothing is selected for its good quality and its ease of use and wear. The dry-cleaning bills would be considered before purchase, and delicate fabrics are seldom bought. The primary purpose of clothing is its versatility and wear, not its artistic merit.

In generational poverty, clothing is usually bought at garage and church sales. If new clothing is purchased, it tends to be worn once and then returned for a refund. To show you love your child, you sometimes buy name-brand clothing even when you can't afford it.

The introduction of casual wear has changed some of the workplace rules. Appearance, however – particularly the choice of clothes – still tends to be used as a key indicator in both hiring and advancement. For one to be promoted to the executive level, it's important that the employee's spouse understand that his/her clothes are *very* important. Molloy recommends that one go to Saks Fifth Avenue, Neiman Marcus, or another upscale store – and find a personal assistant who can help with appropriate purchases.

Energy Level

Another subset of physical resources is the energy level of the individual. People who are physically fit have more energy – and bring it to the workplace. Studies show that a high energy level is one of the best predictors of an entrepreneur's success.

RUBRIC EXPLANATION

0   Cannot take care of physical self. Requires assistance. Risky behaviors create health problems.

Usually these people are not hired. Being clean and wearing clean clothing are required for virtually every job. But even if individuals are clean, they may engage in behaviors that jeopardize their health – e.g., smoking; indiscriminate, unprotected sexual activities; and excessive drinking.

1   Can take care of self. Often sick. *Or* can take care of self but does not. Unkempt.

After getting hired, an employee often comes to work unclean. (We finally needed to tell one of our employees that he *had* to wash his hair.) Clothes are wrinkled and sloppy. Further, if someone is frequently ill, the impact on the workplace in terms of dollars – and in some cases, morale – can be tremendous. Continuity of performance also becomes an issue. Often, in both this and the preceding category, there also are workers who have an emotional or mental illness that hasn't been addressed.

2   Clean, presentable. Able to take care of self. Mostly healthy.

This individual is clean but may need direction regarding appropriate clothing. We had to make a rule that there would be no halter tops and short shorts at work. These employees aren't dependent on anyone else to care for them. And, overall, aside from the occasional flu or heavy cold, they're healthy.

3   Attractive. Physically able. Mostly healthy.

These individuals make work pleasant. Because they're attractive, physically able, and healthy, they enhance the workplace with their dependability and contributions. As has been said before, a major portion of success is simply showing up and being ready to work.

4   Very attractive. Weight, height proportional. Excellent physical health.

These individuals bring energy to the workplace. It may be hard to believe, but research shows that people actually come to look at them and be with them, which brings to mind the line from the old Carpenters song: "Just like me, they long to be, close to you." The research also indicates that these employees make more money than their counterparts. In short, their health and appearance give them vitality – and influence over others.

HOW CAN I USE THIS INFORMATION?

If you have an employee who is dressing inappropriately, you can …	~ explain the company guidelines regarding appearance.
If you or an employee are not being promoted because of appearance, you can …	~ go to an upscale store and get advice. ~ read John Molloy's book *Dress for Success*.
If you wish to encourage physical fitness, you can …	~ develop incentives for participation in gyms, fitness centers, spas, etc.

WHAT DID THE RESEARCH FIND?

Our research did not find a correlation between physical resources and any other resource. Most of the participants gave themselves either a 3 or 4 in this area. A limitation of the study may be that individuals who have significant physical problems may not be working and would not have been part of the study.

CHAPTER

10

WHO TAKES CARE OF ME? WHOM DO I TAKE CARE OF?

SUPPORT SYSTEMS

	0	1	2	3	4
Support system	Alone.	Is providing support for limited group of people, which could include friends or family. Tries to build intimacy at work.	Has support system of friends and family. Friends and family may not know appropriate hidden rules of individual's position.	Has support system at work and at home. Knows how to seek help if needed. Friends and family know appropriate hidden rules of individual's position.	Has support system at home, at work, and in community. Has large network of professional colleagues. Can purchase help if needed.

Support Systems

A support system is a group of friends, family, and institutions that provide money, time, assistance, emotional support, and know-how to an individual. Support systems come both in sensory-based forms and as abstract systems that protect the person (insurance, trusts, and the like).

Support systems cut both ways. The employee may have a strong network of support, or it may be minimal in the extreme. But the employee also may be a key link in a support system for *other* people in his/her life.

The level of a support system can be reflected in net worth. Who stays with the kids when they're sick and can't go to school? Who takes care of Grandma now that she has Alzheimer's? Who spends three hours on the phone getting the property-tax bill straightened out? Who goes grocery shopping? Who buys the holiday gifts? Who cleans the house? Who packs and unpacks the suitcases? Who pays the monthly bills? Who listens when Cindy has a problem? Who takes care of the children while Mom goes to the hospital to have another baby?

These are all part of the support system of workers. Support systems can be purchased in the form of service personnel. But when there isn't enough money to pay for help, then it requires a time investment by friends or family or both.

When an individual is working *and* providing key support for a family, then one or the other becomes the priority. Often, especially for single parents, the family's support system takes precedence. According to the research, single women without children and married men receive the most promotions. Generally they devote the least amount of time to the maintenance of support systems.

How Does the Lack of a Support System Impact Work?

Sally is a bright and quick administrative assistant. Her boss travels quite a bit. Sally is young, has one child, and is married to a man who works a swing shift (three 12-hour shifts on nights, three 12-hour shifts on days, three days off). Sally's boss hired an office manager because there were so many puzzling situations in his absence.

One day Sally begged the office manager for time off in the afternoon, promising that she would return in the evening and make up the two hours she took off in the afternoon. The office manager waited in the evening for Sally; she never returned. When the office manager confronted her the next day, Sally said, "When else but the afternoon could I do the grocery shopping? My husband gets so mad if I'm not there in the evening."

RUBRIC EXPLANATION

0   Alone.

People who are loners, by choice or by circumstance, often have difficulty with relationships – in the workplace and elsewhere.

1   Is providing support for limited group of people, which could include friends or family. Tries to build intimacy at work.

Li and Jiang and their 6-year-old son have moved to Chicago because of Li's job transfer. Li has had the opportunity to help develop a business. Jiang also has a job. Because Li is putting his money back into the business, they are living on Jiang's salary. Money is tight. Both are working 50 to 70 hours a week. Neither has had much opportunity to make friends because of the demands of the jobs. And when they're not working they want to have time with their son. The child-care quality is problematic because their personal budget is tight. Sometimes they both feel so alone. All the relatives are so far away – in San Francisco and China.

2   Has support system of friends and family. Friends and family may not know appropriate hidden rules of individual's position.

Daniel has been promoted to director of Operations. The company he works for is small, but it's growing quickly. He and his wife, Sharon, married when they were both young and poor. One night the owner of the company asks Daniel if he'll meet him at the country club with a prospective client to discuss business. Daniel inquires if Sharon may come along, because he promised to take her out to dinner that evening. The owner says yes. When they enter the country club, the maitre d' asks where they would like to sit. Sharon says, "Let's sit in the smoking section by the band. I love live music!" And so they do, much to the owner's dismay. Not only doesn't he smoke, he dislikes loud music, which makes conversation difficult.

3   Has support system at work and at home. Knows how to seek help if needed. Friends and family know appropriate hidden rules of individual's position.

Anita and Roy met each other after a bitter divorce for each. He was a policeman; she had been an administrative assistant. When they got married, they combined households. Roy eventually left law enforcement and went to work for a company involved in risk management. Anita was repeatedly promoted until she became an office manager. Roy took a job as executive vice president of Risk Management. Anita understands that she needs to change some of her habits and appearance in order to support Roy in his pursuit of an executive career. So, once a month, she drives an hour to a large city to have access to the services of a top-notch hairdresser, manicurist, and pedicurist. Her clothing purchases are now careful and appropriate. She understands and accepts the role she plays in contributing to Roy's success. (Anita also is enjoying the positive comments she has been getting at work about her improved appearance.)

4 Has support system at home, at work, and in community. Has large network of professional colleagues. Can purchase help if needed.

This individual has a lawyer or law firm, a CPA or accountant, a network of doctors, professional colleagues, and political connections, as well as additional supports, including housekeeper(s), administrative assistant, insurance policies (disability, health, life, household, car), yard maintenance services, and repair services (such as air conditioning and electrical).

Furthermore, he/she knows who can be contacted for additional information. It may include private clubs (they can arrange a party at a moment's notice), florist, caterer, domestic help, and limo service.

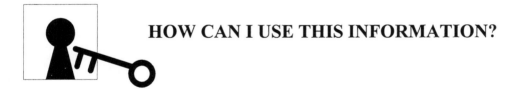 **HOW CAN I USE THIS INFORMATION?**

If you have an employee who does not have a support system, you can …	~ access and provide a list of free social services in the area.
If you have an employee who is a key part of the support system for a group of people, you can …	~ provide links to social service agencies. ~ provide day care as part of the cafeteria plan or company benefits. ~ provide transportation services (as Cascade Engineering of Grand Rapids, Michigan does).

If you wish to have a stronger support system yourself, you can …	~ volunteer in community agencies. ~ start attending meetings of a local religious group or charity. ~ reallocate budget (e.g., pay for a cleaning service every couple of weeks).

WHAT DID THE RESEARCH FIND?

Our research showed that a high score in a support system was positively correlated with a high mental score, a high spiritual score, and a high relationship score. Individuals who had a strong support system also tended to have the other three resources.

CHAPTER
11

THEY CAN
MAKE YOU,
THEY CAN
BREAK YOU

RELATIONSHIPS

	0	1	2	3	4
Relation-ships	Uncommitted relationships that are destructive or damaging.	Few bonding relationships of any kind. Perceives self as unlovable.	Several personal relationships. Has several individuals who can be relied upon for help. Is loved.	Many personal and professional relationships. Is loved *and* has someone to love.	Large number of personal and professional relationships. Has been mentored and has mentored others.

Relationships

To love and be loved is the greatest gift that can be given and received. To care and be cared for is a close second. Regarding the role of significant relationships in the workplace, Dr. James Comer says it best.

> **No significant learning occurs**
> **without a significant relationship**
> **[of mutual respect].**
>
> **– Comer**

Gender vs. Role Identity

At the heart of the issue is identity. Indeed, the stability of relationships over time is linked to identity. Sociologists will tell you that if someone wants to shatter a cultural way of life, all that needs to be done is take away work. Work gives identity because it establishes a role. Though roles continue to evolve, male identity historically has been linked to being a provider, while female identity has been linked to being a caretaker. Today these sociological insights are even more "on target" in the culture of poverty. When work is taken away, male identity shifts to being a fighter and/or lover, and female identity centers more on being a caretaker/rescuer.

When identity shifts from role to gender, then sex (both the activity and manifestation of it) becomes central to identity. For example, it isn't possible to be a "real" man or woman unless you have proof of sexual activity or prowess – i.e., a child, a man, or a woman. When sex becomes central to identity, a great deal of time must be spent on it and the proof of it. In poverty one of the proofs of how "tough" a male is (and how "strong") is the ability to physically fight.

When one's identity is that of a physical fighter, it isn't easy to have anything other than hourly work. Because if one is a fighter, there are times when one has to disrupt the work cycle – either because of hiding from the police or being in jail or having a criminal record.

Reliance on gender for identity is problematic at work, not only because of sexual-harassment litigation, but also because of what a "real" man or a "real" woman will do. For example, a "real" man doesn't do much paperwork or sit behind a desk. A "real" man doesn't go to the country club. A "real" man doesn't get into a tux and dance a waltz. A "real" man punches out an "a--hole"; he doesn't find a way to work with him. A "real" woman doesn't take orders from a "bitch" who only cares about the damn job. A "real" woman takes care of her family and leaves work if necessary to make sure they're OK.

A key question in promotion becomes this: Is the employee's identity one of role or one of gender?

Relationships That Are Nurturing and Caring

Gender identity is coupled with the nature of relationships. In poverty, people tend to be possessions. One of the key issues in promotion is the cost to personal relationships. When someone gets promoted, a period of time follows in which there's a high learning curve. High learning curves require that more time be devoted to acquiring the skills and knowledge base that go with the promotion. Time devoted to learning inevitably takes away from time devoted to relationships.

A key question regarding promotion is this: Can the individual give up relationships for a period of time to pursue the necessary learning?

Mentors

In the workplace, relationships that are nurturing and positive often come in the form of mentorships. Mentors can make a big difference in career success. Further, the research indicates that individuals who have connections to corporate administrators get promoted more often.

How Does One Build Relationships?

Stephen Covey (1989) uses the notion of an emotional bank account to convey crucial aspects of relationships.

DEPOSITS	WITHDRAWALS
Seek first to understand	Seek first to be understood
Keeping promises	Breaking promises
Kindness, courtesies	Unkindness, discourtesies
Clarifying expectations	Violating expectations
Loyalty to the absent	Disloyalty, duplicity
Apologies	Pride, conceit, arrogance
Open to feedback	Rejecting feedback

Taken from *The Seven Habits of Highly Effective People*

What Happens When a Relationship Breaks Apart?

There are five stages one goes through when a relationship breaks apart, according to John Gottman, in his book *Why Marriages Succeed or Fail: And How You Can Make Yours Last*. The first stage is anger; then criticism; then contempt; then silence (which is either physical withdrawal or not speaking); and, finally, separation.

RUBRIC EXPLANATION

0   Uncommitted relationships that are destructive or damaging.

Kitty is 29 and homeless. In the last five years she has had 20 jobs and many lovers. She has a cocaine habit and is now mentally unstable. Most of her teeth are gone. She is often unkempt and dirty. Law enforcement knows her in several communities. Kitty is very bright and has had numerous chances for schooling. But, based on previous patterns, within six months Kitty almost certainly will engage in damaging or self-destructive behavior. No one in her family will take her into their home anymore. They have basically given up on her. Prison or a homeless shelter seems almost inevitable.

1   Few bonding relationships of any kind. Perceives self as unlovable.

Jackson's mother was an alcoholic before she died seven years ago, and his father was distant and away with work. His mother and father divorced, after which his mother had a succession of men through the household. His father remarried, but he and the stepmother didn't get along. A 40-year-old, Jackson was married for a few years in his 20s and has a son, but he has lost track of him. In recent years Jackson has shied away from most relationships, keeping things superficial with both women and men.

2   Several personal relationships. Has several individuals who can be relied upon for help. Is loved.

Richard is 34 and single. He has a good family network. He has 10 siblings and many nieces and nephews. Richard knows there are many family members who would help him at a moment's notice.

3   Many personal and professional relationships. Is loved *and* has someone to love.

Dolores is 58 and married. She has lived in the same community for 50 years. She and her husband go to church every Sunday morning and Wednesday evening. Over the years she has participated in many community activities (the PTO, cancer drive, hospital auxiliary, etc.). She and her husband are planning to travel extensively starting in about five years when they both retire. Her children and grandchildren come to see her or call her regularly. She has a wide circle of friends and family; with Dolores love is a two-way street.

4   Large number of personal and professional relationships. Has been mentored and has mentored others.

Gerald Cooke, a former boss of Ruby's who is now deceased, was the executive director of a regional educational consulting center for 10 years. His network of contacts was statewide, including many political, professional, and personal friends. The number of individuals who attribute their career success – at least in part – to Gerald is phenomenal. He became known throughout the state for his warmth, political genius, integrity, vision, and leadership.

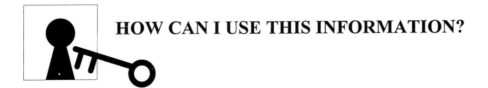 **HOW CAN I USE THIS INFORMATION?**

If you have an employee who needs to develop relationships of mutual respect, you can …	~ teach Stephen Covey's notion of the bank account of relationships. ~ discuss concepts of mutual respect – i.e., respect quickly erodes when one person is always the giver and the other is always the taker.

If you wish to develop stronger relationships of mutual respect, you can …	~ identify the ways in which you provide support to others. ~ identify the support/relationships you need from others.

 **WHAT DID THE RESEARCH FIND?**

Our research indicated that strong relationships were highly correlated with integrity, spiritual resources, and support systems. Further, we found that relationship scores were significantly higher for women than they were for men.

CHAPTER
12

WHY
WON'T
YOU
DO
THIS?

DESIRE

	0	1	2	3	4
Desire and persistence	Low energy. Not motivated. Does not want to be promoted. Dislikes learning. Quits often.	Selective energy but maybe not at work. Works for the money. Does not seek promotion. Avoids training. Gives up easily.	Steady energy. Motivated by need to be personally right. Controls information. Wants to be promoted for the power. Attends training.	High energy. Motivated by need to be organization-ally correct. Seeks out training. Promotion or rewards desired for recognition.	High energy. Motivated by challenge. Promotion or rewards reflect excellence. Constantly learning on his/her own. Very persistent.

Desire and Persistence

The employee can do it. He/she has the resources, the abstract knowledge base. But he/she won't do it. Why? The concept of motivation, or will, enters the picture at this juncture.

A key question regarding promotion is this: Does the person have the desire to succeed?

In our research study, we found that desire was a key factor both in job title and income. For men, there was a direct correlation between growing up in poverty and the drive to succeed. The research study didn't find the same correlation for women who grew up in poverty. Furthermore, the study indicated that men overall had a higher desire/persistence score than women did. The desire/persistence score also was correlated to high integrity, high mental resources, and high spiritual resources.

RUBRIC EXPLANATION

0   Low energy. Not motivated. Does not want to be promoted. Dislikes learning. Quits often.

Delia works only until she has enough time in so she can quit and draw unemployment. She spends as much time as possible playing games on her computer and surfing the Internet. Good at deflecting questions, she's difficult to supervise. Delia usually won't move from her desk except to eat. When work isn't finished, there's always a reason or excuse. She won't use new procedures because "they won't work for me."

1   Selective energy but maybe not at work. Works for the money. Does not seek promotion. Avoids training. Gives up easily.

"As far as I'm concerned, I had to come back to work so I could rest." So said Loren, who lives for racing. His job is only for the money so he can race. At work at the auto parts store, he doesn't want to be promoted. He will often talk to prospective buyers about racing until they leave the store – without purchasing what they came for.

2   Steady energy. Motivated by need to be personally right. Controls information. Wants to be promoted for the power. Attends training.

Tanasia works hard, including overtime. But she frequently leaves early on Friday if she has put in her hours for the week. She is a bookkeeper with a small company. Her work is incredibly accurate. But as the company grows, there are parts of her job that she refuses to train anyone for. She took a two-week vacation and assured her boss that the assistant she was training could do the work. But in reality, she had told her assistant that there are parts of the job the assistant isn't allowed to do. So for two weeks, a large amount of billing doesn't get done. When Tanasia returns and is asked why she hadn't taught her assistant everything, she replies, "Well, that part of the job has to be perfect." She then starts pressing her boss for a promotion and a raise.

3   High energy. Motivated by need to be organizationally correct. Seeks out training. Promotion or rewards desired for recognition.

Carlos is at the corporate level of a non-profit organization. He is very proud of the recognition he received for his service to the agency. He goes to training seminars and looks for the best training for the organization. However, Carlos won't consider anything that doesn't fit into the immediate needs of the workplace – and won't make any decision that isn't "organizationally correct."

Case in point: One of the secretaries sat beneath an air vent that she alleged contained mold and mildew. As her allergies grew worse and worse, she had to go to the doctor once a week for a shot. She complained about the air vent, but nothing was done. Her boss, who was supervised by Carlos, decided that the secretary didn't need to go to the doctor and must work from 8 to 5, as opposed to 7 to 4, which had enabled her to get to the doctor. Carlos backed the secretary's boss. The secretary filed suit with an environmental agency. In the end, the non-profit organization was fined and spent more than a half-million dollars to pay the fine and correct environmental deficiencies.

4 High energy. Motivated by challenge. Promotion or rewards reflect excellence. Constantly learning on his/her own. Very persistent.

These individuals spend years learning something – whether there's corporate support or not. They often don't expect any support. They understand that many times expertise isn't appreciated and, for some, may even be threatening. Most of them read voraciously. Their high energy and stamina last for years. They "push the envelope." They ask such questions as "How can we do this better?" and "What if ...?"

Remember, Thomas Edison made more than 100 light bulbs that didn't work before he found one that did. These individuals seek out training that they think will help them. Their view of rewards is appreciation, but whether there's a reward or not makes little difference regarding their high degree of internally based motivation.

 **HOW CAN I USE THIS INFORMATION?**

If you have an employee who isn't persistent and has low desire, you can …	~ try the following phrases: a. "If you do this, you can win more often." b. "If you do this, you can be in control more often." c. "If you do this, you will be respected more." d. "If you do this, you will not be cheated as often." e. "If you do this, you can give your children more of the things they want/need."
If you have an employee who has high desire and low integrity, you can …	~ identify issues involving choices and consequences. ~ keep that employee away from positions that involve money or supervision.

If you have an employee who is aimless – sometimes motivated and sometimes not – you can …	~ have him/her identify (in writing) weekly goals, as well as long-term goals.
If you wish to increase your own persistence, you can say to yourself …	~ "If I can _____, then I can do this." ~ "This is only two hours out of my life. It won't kill me." ~ "I'll never know unless I try."
If you aren't sure whether something (or someone) is worth the persistence, you can ask yourself …	~ "In five years, will this make a difference in my life?" ~ "Will this make a difference in my life next week?" ~ "Will this impact in a negative or positive way the people I love?" ~ "Will this violate my personal integrity?"

 ## WHAT DID THE RESEARCH FIND?

Finally, in our research study we found that desire was a key factor in both job title and income. There was a direct correlation between men who grew up in poverty and their drive to succeed. The research study did not find the same correlation for women who grew up in poverty. Further, the study indicated that men overall had a higher desire/persistence score than did women. The desire/persistence score also was correlated to high integrity, high mental resources, and high spiritual resources.

CHAPTER
13

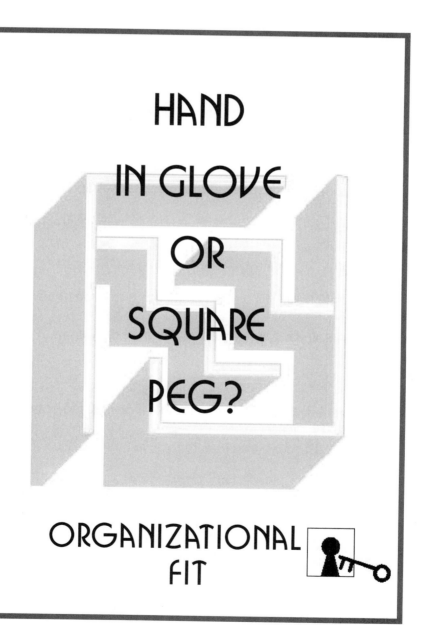

HAND
IN GLOVE
OR
SQUARE
PEG?

ORGANIZATIONAL
FIT

In the introduction, a triangle was introduced.

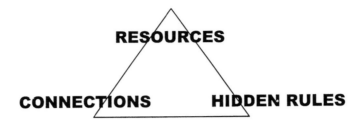

What still needs to be mentioned is that it's not only what an individual brings to an organization, it's also the kinds of attributes that an organization has when a new worker arrives. To be sure, an organization also has its own hidden rules, its own level of resources, and its own networks/connections. Sometimes what the individual brings simply doesn't "fit" with what the organization has. This means a new employee could be all 3's and 4's, start working in an organization, and not be an asset. Indeed, an organization can destroy an individual because the "fit" is so poor.

This book looks at one aspect only – which resources the individual has. But for a true picture to develop, one also must look at the resources of the corporation. For example, if a corporation loses sales, its revenues drop, its key people leave (resulting in a brain drain), the individuals who come in don't have the relationships to leverage so that decisions can be made, then sales drop again, more key people leave, and so forth, until the resources of the organization are so stressed and reduced that the corporation has difficulty surviving.

In other words, the resources of an organization also impact the success of the individual as surely as the individual's resources impact the success of the organization.

CONCLUSION

When we began this book we said that people and organizations have hidden rules – and that those hidden rules can affect the work environment in surprising ways.

So ... what?

Well, understanding those hidden rules – by both supervisor and worker – has everything to do with developing the organization. As you noted in previous chapters, people bring to work all this different "stuff" – and almost always this "stuff" has an impact on their success and their supervisor's success. Ultimately, of course, the organization's success is at stake.

This issue, however, is greater than who does or does not get promoted. It's about the personal and corporate development of intellectual capital, which has been defined as knowledge, applied experience, organizational technology, customer relationships, and professional skills that provide an organization with competitive advantage.

The situation now is simply that intellectual capital is the raw material or resource, both for the individual and the corporation. During the Industrial Revolution raw materials (minerals, oil, timber, etc.) were the foundation of industry. Today the key is intellectual capital – and the individual who is promoted, who is sought after, will see to his/her own development. Wise corporate leaders also will nurture this attribute in their employees.

The organizational world – whether private or public, for profit or not for profit – must make decisions that reflect judgment. The difficult decisions usually are about people. But a limited understanding of "hidden rules" can skew decisions, and that will make a difference in the outcome for an employee, a supervisor, an organization.

Effective change is possible on a foundation built with solid relationships. Though there are people with whom we'd rather not work, we know there are those with whom we must. Some of us have been thrown into close quarters with a brilliant scientist with the mannerisms of a Stone Age hunter. Personality and attitude will always influence how a person's other assets are valued.

In this book we have tried to demonstrate that although you may have an impression of an individual, one might not have a good understanding as to *why* a person does certain things certain ways. In today's team-based environment this understanding is even more vital – and the need for understanding "hidden rules" is more pronounced. Such increased understanding is essential to enhancing communication and to furthering human potential.

When you think about it, intellectual capital (in fact, all capital) originates from people. Whether it's composition, invention, authorship, or process development … the knowledge asset comes from ideas and original thinking.

Even recognizing the value of hard assets, such as natural resources, requires more than a machine.

In order to develop these resources, we must tap into the potential that's available. When people know the "hidden rules" of an organization, there's a tremendous opportunity for them and the organization. Developing this human potential is both necessary *and* a moral obligation!

How do we foster this thinking within our area of responsibility? It does not happen in a vacuum. It does not happen without purpose. Yes, at times the petri dish is accidentally knocked over, thereby revealing a discovery. But even then it will go unnoticed without the right people recognizing the significance. An atmosphere of understanding for and appreciation of the "mosaic" of people is what generates the creative dynamic in organizations. This diverse mix of individuality from many origins and walks of life is what breathes life into any organization.

Why is all this important? It's not about the profit margin. It's not about having a job. It's about surviving – and thriving – for both people and organizations. And it's the world in which our children and our grandchildren will be living.

RESEARCH NOTES

WHAT DOES OTHER RESEARCH SAY?

Hurley, Fagenson-Eland, & Sonenfeld (1997) researched a company that had 270,000 employees worldwide. They looked at its database on top executives from 1970 to 1993. The researchers studied those who got promoted from mid-management to top management positions, as well as those who did not. They found that the following four factors greatly impacted promotion at this level. The individuals who were promoted (1) worked in corporate headquarters and had the opportunity to network with key decision-makers, (2) held a variety of positions, (3) worked in a variety of departments, and (4) remained with the organization for a long time. They found that the following elements were *not* factors in promotion: line positions, years of experience, level of education, gender, and race. It's interesting to note that in their research the race and gender "glass ceiling" exists between the supervisory/management level and the middle-management level.

In a study done by Goodspeed (1997) in the area of financial health care, CEOs were interviewed about key skills they look for in financial executives. They cited the following: executive presence and style, strong interpersonal and communications skills, experience working with boards and public groups, experience in integrated delivery systems, and managed-care contracting experience.

A study done with 300 supervising managers (Moskal, 1995) indicated that the following factors led to promotion: high job performance, engaging more frequently in good corporate/citizenship behavior, being viewed as more committed to the organization, not expressing an intention to leave voluntarily, and having a higher-quality working relationship with their immediate boss.

In another study (Cobb-Clark & Dunlop, 1999), promotions of young workers did not require formal education. However, a little less than half said they felt a need for more training. Promotions seemed to be given to young workers based on their ability to improve their skills.

APPENDIX

RESULTS OF THE KRABILL/PAYNE RESEARCH STUDY

Using Cronbach's Coefficient Alpha Scale, the Krabill/Payne Research Quotient instrument scored .8384 for reliability. A score of .70 is considered good for this type of instrument. The Spearman-Brown formula gives the Krabill/Payne instrument a score of .8955 for reliability. In short, the instrument is reliable.

Of the 250 surveys sent out, 111 were returned, two of which were incomplete. This sampling of people in business targeted the higher end of occupations and income.

In this test, a score of .05 or less (.0500 to .0000) is considered statistically significant. In other words, there is a high probability that there is a strong relationship between the two variables. If one variable is present, the other variable has a high probability of being present as well.

	Integrity	Finan-cial	Emo-tional	Mental	Spiritual	Physical	Support system	Relation-ships	Hidden rules	Desire	Overall score
Job Title	0.009	0.0003		0					0.0002	0	0.00
Gender		*men higher 0.04						*women higher 0.014		*men higher 0.015	
Race											
Years of work											
Years of school											
Class raised in										0.05	
Training									0.0039		
Employers											
Promotions											
Income	0 0045	0		0 0003					0 0002	0 004	0 00

Job titles were grouped in this way: CEO (21), Manager (41), Technical (27), Worker (19), and Retired (5). Only eight of the survey were a race other than Caucasian. Therefore, the number was not great enough for there to be any significant findings by race.

The poorer the individual was growing up, the greater the level of desire and persistence.

There was no difference on overall score due to gender. Women had higher relationship scores than men at a statistically significant level, and men had a higher persistence/desire score than women. In the study 67 of the respondents were men, and 42 were women.

www.ahaprocess.com

	Integrity	Finan-cial	Emo-tional	Mental	Spiritual	Physical	Support system	Relation-ships	Hidden rules	Desire	Promo-tions
Job title											
Gender											
Race											
Years of work		0 4196									0 5355
Years of school											
Class raised in											
Training											
Employers											
Promotions											
Income											

Using the Pearson Product Moment Correlation Coefficients, the above correlations were found: A correlation of .400 or higher (.400 to .999 – positive or negative) is considered significant in that it is higher than a chance occurrence.

	Integrity	Finan-cial	Emo-tional	Mental	Spiritual	Physical	Support system	Relation-ships	Hidden rules	Desire	Overall score
Integrity			0 407					0 4413		0 544	
Financial											
Emotional	0 4073										
Mental							0.4897			0 564	
Spiritual							0 5596	0.4377		0 427	
Physical											
Support system				0 4897	0 5596			0 5339			
Relation-ships	0 4413				0 4377		0 5339				
Hidden rules											
Desire	0 5436			0 5641							
Overall score	0 6756	0 6047	0 602	0 6933	0 6605	0 5841	0.704	0 6463	0.4753	0 734	

Using the Pearson Product Moment Correlation Coefficients, the above correlations were found: A correlation of .400 or higher (.400 to .999 – positive or negative) is considered significant in that it is higher than a chance occurrence.

BIBLIOGRAPHY

By Author

Adler, Ronald B., & Elmhorst, Jeanne Marquardt. (1996). *Communicating at Work, Principles and Practices for Business and the Professions.* New York, NY: McGraw Hill.

Allee, Verna. (1997). *The Knowledge Evolution: Building Organizational Intelligence.* Newton, MA: Butterworth-Heinemann.

Allen, Kelley L. (2000). Manager's tool kit: 'But George, you weren't here.' *Across the Board.* Vol. 37, No. 4. July/August. p. 62.

Anderson, John R. (1996). *The Architecture of Cognition.* Mahwah, NJ: Lawrence Erlbaum Associates, Publishers.

Bennis, Warren. (1989). *Why Leaders Can't Lead.* San Francisco, CA: Jossey-Bass Publishers.

Bennis, Warren. (1997). *Managing People Is Like Herding Cats.* Provo, UT: Executive Excellence Publishing.

Bransford, John D., Brown, Ann L., & Cocking, Rodney R. (Eds.). (1999). *How People Learn: Brain, Mind, Experience and School.* Washington, DC: National Academy Press.

Bridges, William. (1991). *Managing Transitions – Making the Most of Change.* New York, NY: Addison-Wesley Publishing Company.

Brinkman, Rick, & Kirschner, Rick. (1994). *Dealing with People You Can't Stand.* New York, NY: McGraw Hill.

Cassidy, Jim. (1998). The showman who heads the New York Stock Exchange. *Traders Magazine.* Vol. 11, No. 144. October 1. pp. 39-40, 42ff.

Catford, Lorna, & Ray, Michael. (1991). *The Path of the Everyday Hero.* Los Angeles, CA: Jeremy Tarcher.

Caulfield, John. (2000). Home Depot faces bias charge, suit. *National Home Center News.* Lebhar-Friedman, Publisher. Vol. 26, No. 3. February 7. pp. 1ff.

Chadwick, Robert. (1997). Minneapolis, MN: Conflict to Consensus Institute. August 16-18.

Clark, Robyn D. (2000). Has the glass ceiling really been shattered? *Black Enterprise,* Earl G. Graves Publishing Co. Vol. 30, No. 7. February. pp. 145ff.

Cobb-Clark, Deborah A., & Dunlop, Yvonne. (1999). The role of gender in job promotions, *Monthly Labor Review.* Vol. 122, No. 12. December. pp. 32-38.

Cooper, Robert, & Sawaf, Ayman. (1997). *Executive EQ.* New York, NY: Grosset/Putnam.

Costa, Arthur, & Garmston, Robert. (1994). *Cognitive Coaching: A Foundation for Renaissance Schools.* Norwood, MA: Christopher Gordon Press.

Covey, Stephen R. (1989). *The Seven Habits of Highly Effective People: Powerful Lessons in Personal Change.* New York, NY: Simon & Schuster.

Covey, Stephen R. (1990). *Principle-Centered Leadership.* New York, NY: Simon & Schuster.

Covey, Stephen R., Merrill, Roger A., & Merrill, Rebecca R. (1994). *First Things First.* New York, NY: Simon & Schuster.

Crowell, Sam. (1989). A new way of thinking: the challenge of the future. *Educational Leadership.* September. pp. 60-64.

Csikszentmihalyi, Mihaly. (1990). *FLOW: The Psychology of Optimal Experience.* New York, NY: Harper & Row Publishers.

Drucker, Peter. F. (1996). *The Executive in Action.* New York, NY: HarperCollins Publishers.

Drucker, Peter. F. (1996). *The Leader of the Future.* San Francisco, CA: Jossey-Bass Publishers.

Drucker, Peter F. (1998). *Drucker on the Profession of Management.* Boston, MA: Harvard Business School Press.

de Geus, Arie. (1997). *A Living Company.* Boston, MA: Harvard Business School Press.

De Pree, Max. (1989). *Leadership Is an Art.* New York, NY: Dell Trade.

DeSoto, Hernandon. (2000). *The Mystery of Capital.* New York, NY: Basic Books.

Dewey, John. (1933). *How We Think.* Chicago, IL: University of Chicago Press.

Edvinsson, Leif, & Malone, Michael S. (1997). *Intellectual Capital: Realizing Your Company's True Value by Finding Its Hidden Brainpower.* New York, NY: HarperCollins Publishers.

Evans, Patricia. (1996). *The Verbally Abusive* Relationship. Holbrook, MA: Adams Media.

Farr, John. (1997). Sizing up advancement. *Video Store,* Advanstar Communications. Vol. 19, No. 50. pp. 12, 14.

Feuerstein, Reuven. (1988). *Don't Accept Me as I Am.* New York, NY: Plenum Press.

Feuerstein, Reuven, et al. (1980). *Instrumental Enrichment: An Intervention Program for Cognitive Modifiability*. Glenview, IL: Scott, Foresman & Co.

Fisher, John. J. (1999). Holding on to today's employees: The problem isn't kids, it's management (in order to avoid losing good employees, managers need to better understand their Gen X employees). *Medical Marketing & Media*, CPS Communications. Vol. 34, No. 6. June. pp. 60-66.

Fisher, Roger, & Ury, William. (1981). *Getting to YES*. New York, NY: Penguin Books.

Forward, Susan. (1997). *Emotional Blackmail*. New York, NY: HarperCollins Publishers.

Frankl, Viktor E. (1959). *Man's Search for Meaning: An Introduction to Logotherapy*. New York, NY: Beacon Press.

Freeman, Richard B., & Gottschalk, Peter. (Eds). (1998). *Generating Jobs: How to Increase Demand for Less-Skilled Workers*. New York, NY: Russell Sage Foundation.

Gardner, John W. (1990). *On Leadership*. New York, NY: The Free Press.

Garfield, Charles. (1986). *Peak Performers*. New York, NY: Avon Books.

Golonka, Susan. (1998). Strategies to promote education, skill development and career advancement: opportunities for low-skilled workers. Employment and Social Services Policy Studies Division. NGA Reports On-line. July 28.

Goodspeed, Peter W. (1997). *Promotion: A Preparedness Guide*. Washington, DC: Healthcare Financial Management Association. p. 86.

Harrison, Lawrence E., & Huntington, Samuel P. (Eds.). (2000). *Culture Matters: How Values Shape Human Progress*. New York, NY: Basic Books

Hayes, Cassandra. (1998). Life atop the crystal stair. *Black Enterprise*, Earl G. Graves Publishing Co. Vol. 28, No. 7. July. pp. 107-114.

Hayes, James L. (1983). Memos for Management. New York, NY: Amacon.

Heinrich, Carolyn J. (1998). Aiding welfare-to-work transitions: lessons from JTPA on the cost-effectiveness of education and training services. JCPR Working Paper, No. 47. October 1.

Hitt, William D. (1985). *Management in Action*. Columbus, OH: Batelle Press.

Hitt, William D. (1990). *Ethics and Leadership – Putting Theory Into Practice*. Columbus, OH: Batelle Press.

Hitt, William D. (1993). *The Model Leader: A Fully Functioning Person*. Columbus, OH: Batelle Press.

Hitt, William D. (1996). *A Global Ethic – The Leadership Challenge*. Columbus, OH: Batelle Press.

Hurley, Amy E., Fagenson-Eland, Ellen A., & Sonnenfeld, Jeffrey A. (1997). Does cream always rise to the top? An investigation of career attainment determinants. *Organizational Dynamics*. Vol. 26, No. 21. pp. 65-70.

Jensen, Eric. (1994). *The Learning Brain*. Del Mar, CA: Turning Point Publishing.

Kiyosaki, Robert T., & Lechter, Sharon L. (2000). *Rich Dad's Guide to Investing: What the Rich Invest in That the Poor and Middle Class Do Not!* New York, NY: Warner Books.

Klein, Eric, & Izzo, John B. (1998). *Awakening Corporate Soul: Four Paths to Unleash the Power of People at Work*. Lions Bay, British Columbia, Canada: Fairwinds Press.

Kramer, Fredrica, D. (1998). Job retention and career advancement for welfare recipients. Welfare Information Network: Issue Notes. Vol. 2, No. 13. September.

Lathan, Gary. (2000). Employment testing. *HR.Com*. December.

Madell, Robin. (1998). Moving Vans: Pharmaceutical executive taking charge. Healthcare Marketing & Communications Supplement. pp. 31-35.

Maxwell, John. C. (1993). *Developing the Leaders Around You*. Nashville, TN: Thomas Nelson Publishers.

Maxwell, John. C. (1995). *Developing the Leader Within You*. Nashville, TN: Thomas Nelson Publishers.

McGraw, Phillip C. (1999). *Life Strategies*. New York, NY: Hyperion.

Merriam, Sharan B. (1993). *An Update on Adult Learning Theory*. San Francisco, CA: Jossey-Bass Publishers.

Miller, Lawrence M. (1989). *Barbarians to Bureaucrats*. New York, NY: Fawcett.

Moskal, Brian S. (1995). Promotions: who gets them and why. *Industry Week*, Penton Publishing. Vol. 24, No. 5. p. 44.

Mulling, Emory. (1998). How to tell when someone's ready for promotion. *Atlanta Business Chronicle*. Vol. 21, No. 27. December 11. p. A58.

Oakley, Ed, & Krug, Doug. (1991). *Enlightened Leadership: Getting to the Heart of Change*. New York, NY: Simon & Schuster.

O'Dell, Carla, & Grayson, Jackson C. Jr., with Nilly Essaides. (1998). *If Only We Knew What We Know*. New York, NY: Free Press.

Oshry, Barry. (1995). *Seeing Systems. Unlocking the Mysteries of Organizational Life.* San Francisco, CA: Berrett-Koehler Publishers.

Pascarella, Perry. (1984). *The New Achievers.* New York, NY: Free Press.

Payne, Ruby K. (1998). *A Framework for Understanding Poverty* (Revised Edition). Baytown, TX: RFT Publishing Co. (now **aha!** Process of Highlands, TX).

Peters, Tom. (1986). A *Passion for Excellence.* New York, NY: Random House.

Ridley, Matt. (2000). *Genome: The Autobiography of a Species in 23 Chapters.* New York, NY: HarperCollins Publishers.

Robbins, Stephen P., & Hunsaker, Phillip L. (1996). *Training in Interpersonal Skills – Tips for Managing People at Work.* Upper Saddle River, NJ: Prentiss-Hall.

Sapolsky, Robert M. (1998). *Why Zebras Don't Get Ulcers.* New York, NY: W.H. Freeman & Co.

Schwartz, Peter. (1996). *The Long View.* New York, NY: Doubleday-Currency.

Seligman, Martin E.P. (1990). *Learned Optimism.* New York, NY: Alfred A. Knopf.

Senge, Peter M. (1990). *The Fifth Discipline.* New York, NY: Doubleday-Currency.

Shulman, Lee. (1987). Assessment for teaching: an initiative for the profession. *Phi Delta Kappan.* Vol. 69, No. 1. September. pp. 38-44.

Sinetar, Marsha. (1991). *Developing a 21st-Century Mind.* New York, NY: Villard Books.

Spencer, John. (2000). *Who Moved My Cheese?* New York, NY: G.P. Putnam Sons.

Stewart, Thomas A. (1997). *Intellectual Capital: The New Wealth of Organizations.* New York, NY: Doubleday-Currency.

Sveiby, Karl Erik. (1997). *The New Organizational Wealth: Managing and Measuring Knowledge-Based Assets.* San Francisco, CA: Berrett-Koehler Publishers.

Towler, John. (2000). Finding employees with integrity. *HR.Com.* December 18.

Townsend, Robert. (1984). *Up the Organization.* New York, NY: Alfred A. Knopf.

Uchitelle, Louis. (1997). Raises arrive at bottom rung of labor force. *New York Times.* May 23. p. D1.

Ury, William. (1991). *Getting Past NO.* New York, NY: Bantam Books.

Walton, Mary. (1986). *The Deming Management Method.* New York, NY: Perigee.

Weller, Mary, & Barnhart, Rosemary. (1996). Guidelines to establishing a post employment support program including job retention services for newly employed welfare recipients. www.olywa.net/rosemaryb/guidelines.html

Wheatley, Margaret. (1992). *Leadership and the New Science.* San Francisco, CA: Berrett-Koehler Publishers.

Wilson, Edward O. (1998). *Consilience: The Unity of Knowledge.* New York, NY: Alfred A. Knopf.

By Title

Career prospects may be dimmer for unpaid-leave takers. (2000). *HR Focus.* Vol. 77, No. 4. pp. 8-9.

Ex-employees at GM's Hughes Unit win $89.5 million in race-bias case. (1994). *Wall Street Journal* (Princeton, NJ, Edition), Vol. 224, No. 83. October 27. p. B4.

Innovations and products at the Casey jobs initiative sites. Stage 3: advancement. (2000). Baltimore, MD: Annie E. Casey Foundation. June.

Many welfare recipients lack the basic skills needed to succeed in the workplace. Research brief. (1999). Public Policy Institute of California, Issue No. 16. San Francisco, CA. (This brief summarizes a report by Hans P. Johnson and Sonya M Tafoya titled The basic skills of welfare recipients: implications for welfare reform.) April.

People: managing your most important asset (compilation of authors). (1990). Boston, MA: *Harvard Business Review.*

Project match: a research update. (1996). Chicago, IL: Erikson Institute. August.

Retain top staff with improvements in three hiring and training programs. (2000). Accounting Department Management & Administration Report, No. 5. pp. 5ff. New York, NY: Institute of Management & Administration.

Texaco faulted over promotions. (1996). *New York Times* (National Edition). Vol. 145, No. 50459. June 15. p. 15.

www.ahaprocess.com

aha! Process, Inc.
PO Box 727, Highlands, TX 77562-0727
(800) 424-9484; fax (281) 426-8705

ORDER FORM

Please send me:

_____ copy/copies of *Hidden Rules of Class at Work*

Books: 1-4 books $22/each + $4.50 for first book plus $2.00 each
                                   additional book shipping/handling
           5 or more $15/each + 8% shipping/handling

Subtotal: $ _____
Shipping: $ _____
Sales tax: $ _____ (7.75% in Texas)
Total: $_____

UPS SHIP TO ADDRESS (no post office boxes, please):

Name: _____
Organization: _____
Address: _____
_____
Phone: _____ Email: _____

Method of Payment:
PO # _____
Credit card type: _____ Exp: _____
Credit card number: _____
Check: $ _____ Check # _____

Thank you for your order.

For all current products, please see our website
www.ahaprocess.com